Hungerford
A Pictorial History

Bridge Street, c1914

Hungerford
A Pictorial History

Revised and Enlarged Edition

Dr Hugh Pihlens

WEST BERKS BOOKS

First published in 1992

This revised second edition published 2007

Published by West Berks Books Ltd

Copyright © Dr Hugh Pihlens 1992 and 2007

Dr Hugh Pihlens is identified as the author of this work in accordance with Section 77
of the Copyright, Design and Patents Act 1988

A CIP record for this book is available from the British Library

ISBN 978 0 9556571 0 8

Printed and bound in Singapore
by Tien Wah Press

To my wife Lois,

Whose constant encouragement and help with historical research

have made such a major contribution towards the preparation of this book

Preface to the Second Edition

It is now 15 years since the first edition of this book was published. It proved to be very popular and has been out of print for many years. Many people have been encouraging me to produce a reprint, and originally the plan was to do just that – to reprint the first edition. However, when considering this, it became apparent that a large number of the captions needed updating, mostly because modern usage of premises has changed since 1992, because our knowledge of local history has expanded, or in a few cases because small errors needed correcting.

After some discussion with Christopher Cooke of West Berks Books, who has been so helpful in all our deliberations, I have decided that it would be interesting not only to reprint the original 170 photographs, and to update the captions where necessary, but to add an entirely new section to the book, including nearly fifty photographs mostly dating between 1930 and 1990. (With very few exceptions, the first edition showed photographs from before 1930 only).

I am particularly grateful to the many friends who have so kindly helped me to produce this second edition, especially Jack Williams, whose knowledge of 20th century Hungerford history is second to none, and who has kindly proof-read the text; John and Brenda Newton, who share my passion for Hungerford's history; Roger Day, Ron Scott and Fred Bailey. Above all, I am especially grateful to my wife Lois, who has again so willingly helped in every way with research, proof-reading, and loving support.

Forward to the First Edition

I delight in recommending to you this magnificent publication. I applaud the initiative of its publishers, and pay tribute to the untiring effort and enthusiasm of its compiler, Dr Hugh Pihlens.

Since his arrival in the town some 19 years ago, Hugh's love of his subject has led him to publish in 1983 his own book, *The Story of Hungerford*, besides which he became the instigator of the Hungerford Historical Association, becoming its first Chairman, to be followed in this role later by his wife Lois. This flourishes today, in ever increasing importance and has become one of the town's most highly prized societies. During the intervening years the Pihlens have amassed a large collection of historical data on our town. It is not surprising, therefore, that Hugh should have been asked to compile this latest exciting volume. I endorse his remarks and gratitude to those other members of our community who have provided information and many photographs for inclusion, opening up their own prize collections and in many instances revealing, possibly for the first time, several unique views of this ancient town and inhabitants.

Hungerford is rightly proud of its heritage and traditions, which stretch back through the mists of time. For over six centuries this small town has jealously guarded its ancient rights and privileges, and largely conducted its own affairs. Its unique setting, within large areas of common land, in a beautiful corner of western Berkshire, is widely acknowledged. Its ancient High Street, and other picturesque corners of the town, are cherished by its inhabitants.

This marvellous collection of photographs will therefore find favour and a welcome spot upon the book-shelves of those who live within its bounds. I am confident also that it will portray to the casual visitor, the tourist and the historian, a very real picture of the town, its people, and its fabric of life over a period of many years - and give some clear indication to all of the great pleasure that is derived from being a Hungerfordian.

John L. Newton

Constable of Hungerford 1972-74, and 1991-92

Forward to the Second Edition

The widely acclaimed success of Dr Hugh Pihlens' Pictorial History has resulted in this second edition being produced. This 'updated' edition contains not only the magnificent collection of photographs portraying this fascinating and historic town over a period of many years which was contained in the first edition, but also a significant number of others, many of which are previously unpublished.

I am confident that this latest volume will give immense pleasure to the reader, not only to the more elderly of this town and locality, who will look back on the subject with an air of nostalgia, but also those further afield who cherish our heritage. It will also serve to illustrate that, in this modern and fast-moving world, this little town of ancient origins is not immune from change – all the more reason then for those of today to be guardians of our past.

John L. Newton

List of Illustrations

Cover: The Market Place, c1903 and 2007
Page 2: Bridge Street, c1914

List of Illustrations

List of Illustrations

Illustration Acknowledgements

I wish to thank the following people for allowing me to borrow their photographs and postcards, and for giving me permission to reproduce them in this book. Old photographs are often prized possessions and, without the generosity of the many owners, this book would not have been possible. Within the limits of one book, it is not possible to cover every aspect of the town's history. I trust, however, that readers will find that the final choice does include an interesting and wide variety of subjects.

In addition to the people listed below, there are many others who have kindly loaned photographs which could not be selected because of pressure of space. To them, and everyone who has helped in the production of the book, I extend my sincere thanks:

John Allen, 156; Mrs Janet Cleverley, 72, 74-76, 78, 90; Roger Day, 180, 182; Mrs Marjorie Eatwell, 9, 18, 79, 86, 103, 104, 109, 112, 149; Mrs Beatrice Goodman, 129; Ken and Liz Hall, 196-197; Stewart Hofgartner, 3, 27-29, 58, 130, 136, 143, 155; Mrs Barbara Hope, 8, 20, 37, 65, 113, 115, 162; Dr Humphrey Hope, 10, 68, 80, 158, 159, 163-66, 168, 170; Mrs Sue Hopson, 34, 35, 93, 100, 107, 128, 150, 160; Mrs Freda Horwood, 97, 134; Hungerford Historical Association archives, 186, 187, 193, 198, 199, 211, 212, 218; Col Donald Macey, 22, 41, 47-49, 51, 52, 89, 101, 102, 106, 131, 132, 135, 140; John Miles, 210; Miss Betty Munford, 21, 61, 83, 92, 116, 125, 147; John and Brenda Newton, 57, 88, 117-21, 139, 176, 214-216; Mrs Rosemary Oldfield, 12, 16, 38, 63, 108; Our Lady of Lourdes Catholic Church archives, 185; Darren Prestoe, 19; Hungerford Primary School, 146, 148; Miss Ann Rivers, 32, 39, 56, 77, 87, 91, 96, 98, 127, 154; Ron Scott, 17, 31, 33, 42, 145, 177, 179, 183, 195, 202, 204, 206, 207; Mrs Doris Taylor, 26, 60, 81, 82, 84; Mrs Val Troke, 137; Robin Tubb and family, 13, 14, 30, 36, 53, 54, 62, 122, 123, 141, 144, 167; George Willett, 25, 66, 94; Jack Williams, 181, 188, 189, 200, 203, 217.

Pictures supplied by the author: 1, 2, 4, 5, 7, 11, 15, 23, 24, 40, 43-46, 50, 55, 59, 64, 67, 69-71, 73, 95, 99, 105, 110, 111, 114, 124, 126, 133, 138, 142, 151-53, 157, 161, 169, 171-175, 178, 184, 190-192, 194, 201, 205, 208-209, 213, 219.

My thanks are also due to the many people who have contributed background information for the book. The owners of the photographic originals listed above have in many cases provided historical comments on their photographs, but other contributors include Chris Carlon (re Catholic Church); Paul Lacey (re GWR bus service); Mrs Ruth Lewington (re Albert Parsons); the National Motor Museum, Beaulieu (re Mr Parsons' car); the Shuttleworth Collection (re the Bristol Prier aeroplane).

Introduction

The attractive rural market town of Hungerford is at the very western end of Berkshire, near the borders with Wiltshire and Hampshire. It lies in the North Wessex Downs Area of Outstanding Natural Beauty. A walk around the town and its immediate surrounding countryside will reveal the inherent charm of the area. Much of the town has remained unaltered for generations.

Archaeological excavations on the northern outskirts of Hungerford in 1989 revealed Stone Age tools and the site of a Bronze Age ceremonial building. A Roman road passes just north of the town on its way from Silchester and Speen in the east through Littlecote estate to Mildenhall and Bath in the west. This early information begins the jigsaw of local history, but little of real detail can possibly be known about the town until written records begin.

The Domesday Survey, carried out by King William I in 1086, does not name Hungerford, although many of the manors immediately adjacent to the town are recorded, including Eddington, Leverton, Inkpen, Denford, Avington, Inglewood and Charlton. For the first written evidence of the town, one has to wait just a few years more until c1108, when a document refers to Robert de Beaumont granting 'a manor near Hungerford, Edenetona by name' to the church of the Holy Trinity at Beaumont in Normandy. A community with the name Hungerford clearly existed by this date – probably carved out of a portion of the manor of Kintbury. By 1147 there are records of a parish church at Hungerford, which appears to have been in existence for some years previously. Of this church there are no remains, but there is a beautiful Norman church standing today in an idyllic setting at Avington, just a mile or so east of Hungerford.

The present parish church of St Lawrence was built in 1816, and stands on the site of an Early English predecessor. It is probable that, in turn, this church had been built on the site of the earlier Norman building. The church lies several hundred metres to the west of the town centre. In Norman times it is likely that the village was clustered around the church, on land now known as The Croft, and spreading on to Freeman's Marsh.

Around the end of the 12th century, a new town plan was conceived. This consisted of a main street running roughly north south, with back lanes on either side of the main street, about a hundred metres to the east and west. The area contained within this framework was divided into narrow burgage plots, and within these the new town of Hungerford was built. The overall structure is still visible today, although sadly only a few of the High Street properties retain their long gardens reaching back to Prospect Road in the west, and Fairview Road in the east.

Through the 11th to 14th centuries the manor of Hungerford passed between the Crown and various Duchies of Leicester and Lancaster. In 1351 it was in the ownership of Henry, Duke of Lancaster, who married Isabel of Beaumont. Henry died in 1361 leaving no sons, but two daughters, Maud and Blanche. Maud inherited the estates, but died childless on 10 April 1362: and the manor of Hungerford, along with many other estates, passed to her younger sister, Blanche, wife of Edward III's fourth son, John of Gaunt. This date is therefore of some interest to Hungerfordians.

The connection with John of Gaunt is remembered today in the naming of some important buildings, such as the John of Gaunt Inn and the John O'Gaunt Community Technical College, as well as in street names such as Lancaster Square and Lancaster Close.

Chief of the traditions surrounding Hungerford's association with John of Gaunt is that he granted the right of fishing on the River Kennet from Eldren Stubb (just below Leverton in the west) as far as Irish Stile (at least two miles below Kintbury in the east). To support this tradition there is in the town's possession an ancient (and battered!) brass horn, which is said to have been given to the town by John of Gaunt as guarantee of those rights. There was a written charter confirming these rights, but the Duchy copy was lost in a fire at John of Gaunt's Savoy Palace in The Strand in 1381, and the town's copy was allegedly stolen in the days of Queen Elizabeth I. The loss of the charter occurred when there was increasing hostility between the Duchy and the townspeople over various rights and privileges. Many legal wrangles ensued, and at one stage the town appealed to the Queen herself in an attempt to win the day.

In the reign of James I, the long-standing legal disputes were settled, and in 1612 the King granted the Manor of Hungerford to two local men, John Eldred and William Whitmore. After a further few years of legal transfers, the Manor of Hungerford was conveyed in 1617 to Ralph Mackerell (Constable), and 13 other local men 'in trust for the inhabitants'. These 14 men thus became the first feoffees or trustees of the Town and Manor of Hungerford. The present commoners are those people owning and living in the properties established at the time of the 1612 James I grant.

The organisation of the Town and Manor of Hungerford has been handed down from generation to generation for nearly 400 years. The Commoners' Court is headed by the Constable, who is ably supported by a group of other officials including the Port-Reeve, Bailiff, four Tutti-men, a number of Water-Bailiffs, several Overseers of the Common (Port Down), three Keepers of the Keys of the Common Coffer, two Ale-Tasters (or 'Testers'), and the Bellman and Assistant Bailiff. Some offices have fallen from usage, including the Searchers and Sealers of Leather, and the Tasters of Flesh and Fish!

The most important day in the life of the Town and Manor is Tutti-Day, always held on the second Tuesday after Easter. In the past this was the day by which all quit rents and fines were due to be paid, and it marks the end of the financial and administrative year. The Bellman (who is also Town Crier) summons all the Commoners to the Commoners' Court, which is held in the Town Hall at 9 o'clock. Meanwhile the two Tutti-men, accompanied by their guide and mentor, the Orangeman, work their way around the town, visiting every house with common rights, numbering nearly 100 in total. In the past they would have collected the 'head penny' from each householder, but nowadays the most they collect is a kiss from the ladies of the house, and a little hospitality to help them on their way.

Meanwhile, in the Town Hall, the Commoners' Court is under way. The Constable guides the Court through a series of stages which are carried out today much as they have been for generations. The officers are elected for the coming year, the accounts are read and agreed, and a number of other matters are discussed concerning the affairs of the Town and Manor.

In 1908 the Town and Manor became a registered charity, and is thus responsible to the Charity Commissioners. The present trustees and court have a considerable responsibility, managing the Town Hall (probably the only Town Hall in the country not paid for by the Council Tax), the John of Gaunt Inn, the Common, Freeman's Marsh, as well as the extensive fishing on the Rivers Kennet and Dun.

In 1688 a very important part of British history took place in Hungerford. The Catholic King James II was King of England, but he was not widely popular, and by 1688 there were plans to remove him from the throne. The Protestant Prince William of Orange landed at Brixham in Devon, and travelled with his army towards London, hoping to gather support for his cause along the way. When the King learned of this approach, James II sent three commissioners to meet Prince William. The meeting took place in the Bear Inn at Hungerford on 6 December 1688, and it was during this meeting that plans were made for the throne of England to pass to William. The very fact that such a crucial meeting took place in Hungerford is evidence, if any were necessary, of the importance of the London to Bath Road, one of the major routes of the country. The fact that Hungerford lay on the Bath Road had a considerable effect on the town's growth and development. Coaching became big business, and Hungerford became a coaching town.

As early as 1228 there are written records of an important road running east-west through Savernake Forest. This 'King's Way' was the forerunner of the Bath Road, and it crossed the River Kennet at the 'pons de Hungreford', recorded in 1275. Savernake Forest was much larger then, and surveys of the forest describe it as extending as far as 'the house of lepers at Hungerford'. In 1232 the Priory of St John was established on land at the northern edge of the town, now the site of Bridge Street. The priory was dissolved by Henry VIII in 1548.

During the Elizabethan period road travel began to be used more widely; one of the Queen's coachmen is known to have been buried in the parish churchyard in 1601. By 1740 traffic along the Bath Road had increased greatly, and at this time the access to the town from the Bath Road was improved. The ford through the River Dun (adjacent to the present war memorial) was proving very inadequate, and land was bought in order to build a new road with bridges — now the northern end of Bridge Street.

Hungerford lay not only on the Bath Road (running east-west) but also on the Oxford to Salisbury turnpike (running north-south). During the hey-day of the coaching period, at the end of the 18th century and the first few decades of the 19th century, the town grew and prospered. There were many coaching inns around the town servicing the coaching trade, along with many stables and blacksmiths. A new Town Hall was built in 1786, and many of the timber-framed High Street properties were 'modernised' by the addition of new Georgian frontages.

The prosperity of the town was further enhanced by the opening of the Kennet and Avon Canal in 1810. Hungerford wharf was a busy trading centre, and brought valuable business to the town. Census figures show that the population rose from 1,987 in the year 1801 to 2,696 in 1851, a very considerable growth of 35 per cent. There seems little doubt that this first half of the 19th century was Hungerford's busiest, but the opening in 1841 of Brunel's Great Western Railway from London via Swindon to Bristol spelt disaster to the canal trade. Journeys that had taken more than a week by canal could now be accomplished in just a few hours. Both the canal trade and coaching traffic slumped.

It seemed that only one thing could help Hungerford - the building of a railway to the town. This came sooner than many would have dreamed of, and a terminus station was opened (on the site of the present station) in 1847. This line was later extended (in 1862) onwards to the west, and one could have expected that Hungerford would continue to thrive, now that it lay on a main railway route. The expected prosperity failed to materialise, however. Rather than bringing trade to the town, the railway drained the town of people and resources. The population actually fell between the years 1851 and 1901.

Despite the many problems at the time, Hungerford's civic pride ran high. A grand new Town Hall and Corn Exchange were built, and several new churches. Two important iron foundries provided employment for many men in the town, and with the continuing role of market town for the local area, Hungerford reached the 20th century as a busy and active community. The Hungerford Water Works was established in 1903, and mains drainage in 1909. Telephones were installed in 1907, a splendid new all-age Council School was built in 1910, and a new post office in 1914. Many of the photographs in this book date from the early 20th century, and the atmosphere of the town can be assessed through them.

The outbreak of the First World War had a profound effect on the town. Many men went to fight, whilst the town itself was host to an army unit assembling here before joining the front. The years after the First World War saw the town begin its great 20th-century expansion. Until that time there had been very few houses outside the main streets of High Street, Bridge Street, Cow Lane (Park Street) and Church Street. Post-war, however, there was an accelerating expansion. This was a time of great community spirit, with a strong emphasis locally on sports and games. A sports ground in The Croft was opened in 1921, and bowls, croquet, tennis, shooting, rugby, football and cricket all thrived. There was even a golf course on the Common.

The Second World War brought huge numbers of mainly American troops to various air bases around Hungerford, including Ramsbury, Membury and Welford. Hungerford train station was very busy, and the town was full of servicemen. The Kennet and Avon canal was a line of secondary defence, and numerous pill-boxes and tank traps were installed in and around the town. Despite the rationing and hardships of the wartime, the people of Hungerford were very generous in fundraising for the war effort.

After the war, the town slowly resumed its normal peacetime activities, and carnivals and sports gradually restarted. The John O'Gaunt school was built, and an open-air swimming pool.

The building of the M4 motorway (which opened on Boxing Day 1971) has brought great prosperity to the whole Kennet Valley, and each decade has brought more housing to Hungerford. Modern Hungerford is well known for its antique shops, and as a tourist centre. The Kennet and Avon Canal was restored at Hungerford in 1974, and fully reopened by The Queen in August 1990. It provides enjoyment for many, whether in boats or on the tow-path.

In the middle of a sunny day on Wednesday 19th August 1987 an event took place in Hungerford that was to have national repercussions. A young man called Michael Ryan began a shooting frenzy that was to leave 16 people dead, and many others seriously wounded. Within just a few hours Ryan had shot himself, but those few hours changed many families in Hungerford, and changed the world. Memorials to those who died were placed both in St Lawrence's Church and at the special memorial on a site near the World War II Memorial Ground in Bulpit Lane. Gradually a healing of the town took place, and it is probably true that most visitors think little about those events twenty years ago. Those who lived in Hungerford at the time will never forget, but are pleased to live in a community that supported itself so closely through such a difficult time.

The photographs in this book cover the whole photographic period from 1850 to the present day, although most date from 1900 to 1920. We are fortunate to have had some excellent photographers in Hungerford and the surrounding area. Foremost of these was Albert Parsons, who came to Hungerford in 1902, and worked here until his death in 1950. The high quality of his work and the large range of photographs he took provide us with a splendid record of the period. Mention should also be made of William Softley Parry, a toy dealer and photographer in Bridge Street in the 1870s. Two of a fine set of early Cartes de Visite dated c1875 showing views around Hungerford are used in this book. Other Hungerford photographers include William Mapson of Church Street and High Street, and Samuel Hawkes of High Street.

In 1907 the Reading photographer Phillip Collier began his photographic record of Berkshire, and several examples are included. Other visiting photographers making important contributions to the Hungerford photographic records include Francis Frith, Benjamin Stone, whose large series of photographs dated 1902 exists, and Charles Hawker of Newbury. During the First World War, the firm of J Templeman of Stoke-on-Trent took the official photographs of the army unit here, but at the same time took some other local views.

Among them all, their photographs provide a very complete record of life in the town at that time. The results these early photographers achieved were all the more remarkable when one considers the equipment and materials they were using. As we enjoy the fruits of their handiwork, we must be grateful for their care and artistic skills, and thankful also to the many people who have kept or collected local photographs over the years.

Sources and Bibliography

Directories:

Universal British, 1792
Berkshire, 1796
Pigot & Co, 1823 and later
Kelly, 1847 and later
Billing, 1854 and later
Post Office, 1869 and later
Cosburn, 1883 and later

Census data, 1801 and later
Commoner's Lists, 1781 and later
Quit Rent Rolls, 1470 and later

Cannon, P, *A Directory of Photographers*, Newbury & District 1854-1945 (1991)
Day, Roger, *Ramsbury At War* (2004)
Day, Roger, *Savernake At War* (2007)
Historical Record of 180 Company RASC (1920)
Hungerford Historical Association, *Hungerford – A History* (2000)
Lewis, Peter, *Squadron Histories* 1912-59 (1959)
Norris, Geoffrey, *The Royal Flying Corps - A History* (1965)
Pihlens, Dr H L, *A Walk About Hungerford* (1988)
Pihlens, Dr H L, *The Story of Hungerford* (1983)
Summers, The Rev W H, *The Story of Hungerford in Berkshire* (1926)
Williams, Jack, *A Man of Hungerford – The Memories of Jack Williams*, (2002)

List of Photographers and Publishers, with Dates of Local Plates

Ernest Barnard, Hungerford, 1906-18 : 26, 66, 74, 89, 98
Alfred Barratt, Fleet Street, London, 1911 : 51
Chester Vaughan, 1903-8 : 25
Phillip Collier, Reading, 1907 : 40 - 41, 68, 87, 107, 114, 128, 133, 136, 154
Elliott and Fry, London, 1910 : 152
Freeman's lithographic series, 1903 : 3, 27-29, 94
Freeman's photographic series, 1910 : 9
Charles Hawker, Newbury, 1883-1937 : 143, 155
A W Hoare, Reading, 1930 : 52
Frederick Jessett, Eddington, 1907-8 : 109, 113
William Mapson, Hungerford and Pewsey, 1898-1905 : 60, 135
William Softley Parry, Bridge Street, Hungerford, 1876-83 : 57, 139
Albert Parsons, Hungerford, 1902-50 : 10, 12, 14-21, 23, 30, 31, 33-39, 43-50, 53-56, 59, 63, 69-71, 74-79, 84-86, 92, 93, 96, 100, 108, 112, 115, 122-27, 129, 131, 140, 141, 146, 147, 151, 156-170, 200, 213
J Benjamin Stone, 1902 : 144
J Templeman, Stoke-on-Trent, 1914-1918 : 61, 81, 82
W. Wicks, Hayes, Middlesex, 1910 : 153
Wyndham Series, c1904 : 32, 40

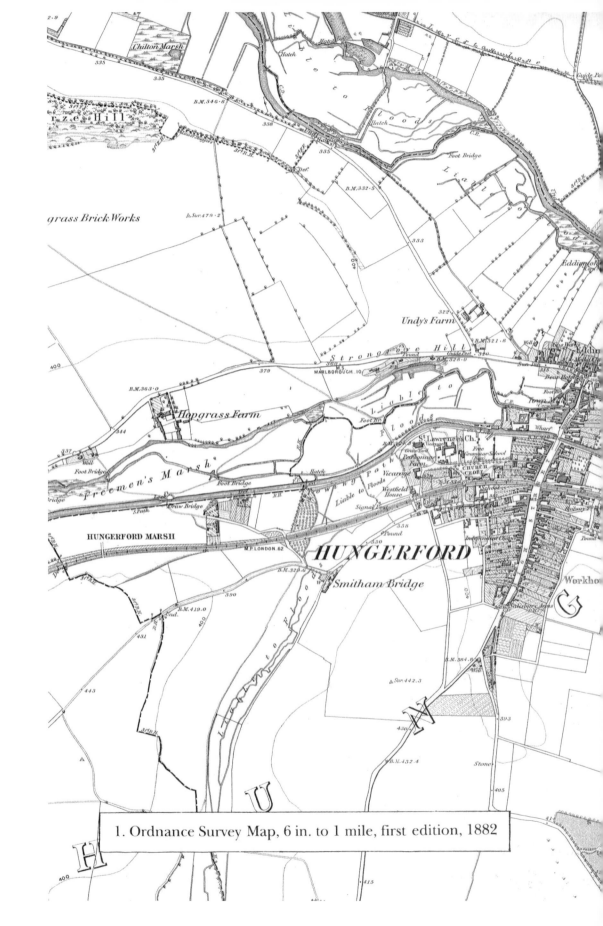

1. Ordnance Survey Map, 6 in. to 1 mile, first edition, 1882

The Bear Hotel

2. The Bear Corner, c1910

This scene is familiar to everyone who has travelled the Bath Road.
On the right is the Bear Hotel, a coaching inn whose origins date
back to the 13th century. There are written records surviving from
1464. It was here that the commissioners of King James II met
Prince William of Orange in 1688 before he claimed the Crown of
England. Riverside House (now Great Grooms Antiques and Fine
Paintings) stands proudly overlooking the scene, whilst on the left
are Charlie Batchelor's furniture shop, and Jessett's bakery (now
private houses).

The Town Halls and the Market Place

3. *right:* **The Town Hall, c1902**

Hungerford's Town Hall Corn Exchange is an imposing building in the Market Place. Posters on the outside advertise film shows which were held in the Corn Exchange until the Regent Cinema opened at the top of Atherton Hill (see plates 183 and 184). On the left is the Crown Brewery, run by Elisha Love, shown here just before the addition of a mock-Tudor frontage. The foundation stone of the Town Hall had been laid in 1870 by Mr Cherry of Denford Park (see plate 29), whose portrait hangs in the hall.

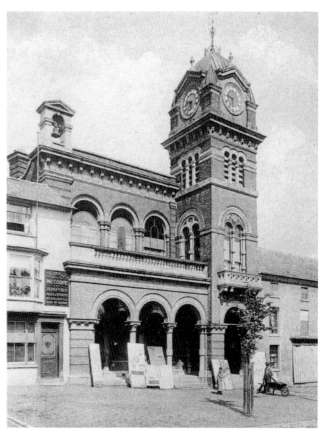

4. *below:* **Olde Town Hall, 1862**

Hungerford has had at least four town halls. The first, perhaps dating back to the time of John of Gaunt in the 14th century, was recorded in a survey by the Duchy of Lancaster of 1543/4 as being 'ruinous and utterly dekeyed'. In 1607 a new town hall was built, which was to last until the late 1700s. This early glass plate shows the third town hall, built 1786, standing in the middle of the market-place, and surmounted by its octagonal cupola. Spanning the High Street beyond the Town Hall is Hungerford's original railway bridge, built in 1862 to carry the railway further west. This bridge was later replaced in 1896 by the lattice bridge seen in several other photographs in this book.

5. *above:* **The Town Hall and Market Place, June 1862**

Mr Hall, the Magistrate's Clerk, gave to the town a grand four-faced clock. To accommodate it, a new clock-tower was built on the Town Hall in 1862 replacing the earlier (and better proportioned) cupola, seen in the previous photograph. Opposite the Town Hall can be seen (from left to right) the Three Swans Inn (now Three Swans Hotel), the Bell Inn (now Fare Wise Travel), and Edwin Wiggins, blacksmith (later Charles Oakes, and now Nye & Co, estate agents). To the right of Cow Lane (now Park Street) is the Plume of Feathers Inn, and Bodman's drapery store (until recently Age of Elegance).

6. *below:* **The two Town Halls, 1871**

For a few months only there were two Town Halls in Hungerford. In the foreground is the 1786 building. Its clock-tower is empty, the clock having been transferred to the tower of the newly-built Corn Exchange behind. Between January and April 1872 the building was demolished, some of the materials being used to build cottages in Church Street.

The Church, The Croft and the Old Town Layout

7. Print of Hungerford church, c1813

The parish church of Hungerford stands, somewhat unusually, well away from the centre of the town. It was first mentioned in a document dated 1147, and that original building was replaced by one in the early English style during the 13th century. By the early 1800s this building had become so dilapidated that it was in danger of falling down. In 1811 major repairs were undertaken, but as soon as the work was completed, part of the original building collapsed bringing with it the newly completed tower. This print shows the crumbling church and tower, its bell now removed to a wooden gantry under the trees on the left.

8. The parish church and the canal, 1903

When the early English church collapsed, there was clearly no alternative but to build a completely new church. In 1814 an Act of Parliament was obtained, authorising the vicar, churchwardens and trustees to raise £6,000 for the task. In the end the new church was to cost £30,000, the balance being raised partly by private donations, and partly by a tontine, a form of cumulative insurance rarely heard of nowadays. The remaining portion of the old church was demolished, and in its place a new Georgian Gothic building was erected, designed by Mr Pinch of Bath, and consecrated on 30 August 1816. Standing so close to the canal which was opened just a few years earlier in 1810, it is not suprising that it was built in Bath stone.

9. The church gate, c1910

To celebrate the completion of the restoration, a set of new gates
was installed at the churchyard entrance. These double gates, with
adjacent kissing gate, were donated by the Town and Manor of
Hungerford in 1886. The gas lamps seen in this photograph were
replaced in 1940 by an electric light on an arch over the gateway,
a gift of Mr and Mrs Astley.

10. The Vicarage, c1920

Standing adjacent to the churchyard is the Vicarage, dating from the 17th century. The Vicarage stands very close to the canal, and in order to keep his three children safe when playing in the garden, the vicar sometimes tethered them to trees. One bishop commented after visiting the vicar: 'Hungerford is the only place I know where the children are tied up, and the dogs are loose'!

11. The Church Croft, c1895

The Croft is a quiet green away from the hustle and bustle of the High Street. It is said that the Church Croft was given to the town by John Undewes and his wife for 'a place to sport therein' at the nominal rent of a red rose yearly if demanded. Such a rent is not demanded, and The Croft is now part of the Town and Manor land. It was in this area surrounding the church that the original village of Hungerford probably stood, until the new town plan was laid out at the end of the 12th century. On the left is a tiled building clearly recognisable as the present day Hungerford Club House. The thatched cottages beyond have been demolished, but the tiled and gabled cottage in the distance still stands (1 The Croft).

12. Church Croft Avenue, c1911

The straight roadway running along the northern edge of The Croft, joining Little Church Lane (now Church Lane) and the church, was known as Croft Avenue. The avenue was lined by some very tall elm trees. They had been planted c1840 to replace an earlier avenue. The children help to show how tall the trees had become.

13. *below:* The Croft, c1890

One's eye is immediately drawn to the children in this photograph, standing carefully positioned for best effect. Perhaps the most special feature of this early print, however, is that it is one of the rare photographs showing the old Free Grammar School established by the Rector of Welford, the Rev Thomas Sheaffe, in 1635. It is the building to the right of the trees in line with the church tower. The Grammar School existed until 1884 and the building was eventually demolished to make way for the Church House in 1900 (see plate 16).

14. Sweet chestnuts in The Croft, 1913

The trees shown in plates 12 and 13 eventually became too tall and needed replacement. In 1913 an avenue of young sweet chestnuts was planted. On the left, in the bowler hat, is Mr Henry d'Oyley Wolvey Astley, the local solicitor and Clerk to the Town and Manor. Despite the slow shutter speed blurring the ferocious activity of the digger, we know that the new trees were planted by the Constable, Mr John Adnams. His wife, Mrs Ginny Adnams is said to have been unhappy about the choice of sweet chestnuts, feeling that they were unlucky and unsuitable. She purchased her own tree, a copper beach, and planted it in front of St. Lawrence's church gate. It was a beautiful tree, but died c1980, and was replaced by a London plane.

15. The Croft, c1913

With the felling of the old trees, The Croft assumed a fresh and less oppressive air. The old tracks across The Croft can clearly be seen, with St. Lawrence's church and the Church House in the background.

16. Church House, c1911

After the Grammar School had closed in 1884 (see plate 13), the site was sold in November 1898 to Sir William George Pearce (of Chilton Lodge, see plate 26), who built the Church House (now Croft Hall) in 1900. Sir William Pearce gave the premises to the town, along with an endowment in his will. Church House was used as a library, for the Sunday School, and by the Church House Club (formed in 1901) before the bowling green, croquet lawn and tennis courts were developed in 1921.

17. Church House sports section, 1923

The sports ground was laid out on land between The Croft and the canal. The plan was different from the modern layout, and two tennis courts can be seen on the site of the present-day bowling green. In the background can be seen the cottages at Strongrove Hill (including the ruins of one razed by fire). The three tall poplar trees are adjacent to Hungerford canal lock.

Sports Clubs

18. Married v Single, 1921

The 1920s were years when sport features strongly in the life of
Hungerford. Teams and matches were arranged with almost every
combination imaginable. This photograph shows the teams taking
part in the annual Football Club match between the married and
single men. The teams are posed in front of what became the cricket
pavilion – which is the old GWR Savernake station re-used! Good
classic GWR style. A later cricket pavilion (which burnt down in
1963) was made from re-cycled packing cases that were used to
transport the Waco gliders from the USA during the Second
World War.

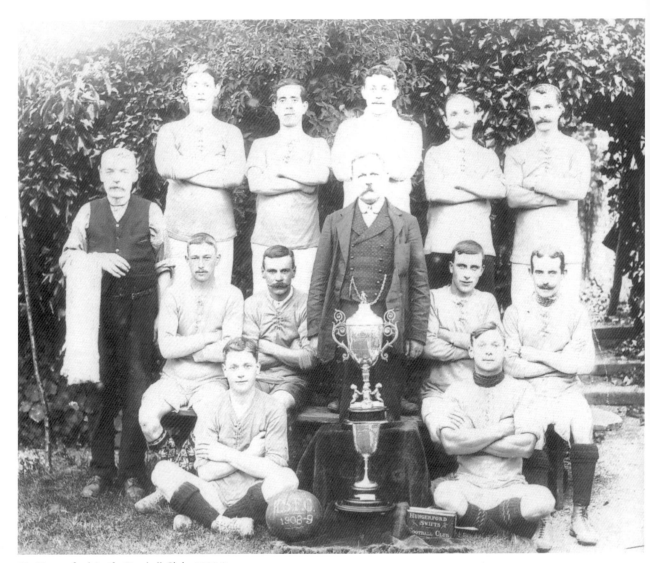

19. Hungerford Swifts Football Club, 1908-9

The Football Club at this time was on the western edge of the town
beyond Smitham Bridge, near The Orchard in Marsh Lane.

20. Ladies v Gents cricket, 1913

The Cricket Club, under the captaincy of the Rev John Denning (see plate 23), played many local elevens. In August each year there was always good support for the Ladies v Gents match, when the men played with a bat more suitable to rounders than cricket!

21. Lancastrian Tennis Club, 1914

Before tennis courts were made in The Croft, tennis was played at the Lancastrian Tennis Club, on what is now the Primary school field, off Fairview Road. In the background you can see the Council school building, opened in 1910 (see plate 146).

22. *above:* **Astor Challenge Rifle Cup, 21 June 1906**
The Hungerford and District Rifle Club won the Astor Challenge Cup (Berkshire County) in 1906. The team members and their scores were: W Blake (Capt), 84; E Clements, 83; W Chapman, 82; A Bartholomew, 77; A Macklin, 78; and P Jessett, 72; Total, 476. The result was a tight one, with the other teams scoring as follows: Wokingham 475; Windsor, 440; Reading, 428; Newbury Guildhall, 427; and Bucklebury, 209. Poor Bucklebury – not a good day!

23. *left:* **The Rev John F Denning, MA, c1921**
In addition to being curate of Hungerford from 1889 to 1895, Mr Denning was headmaster of Westfield House school in Parsonage Lane from 1893 until it closed c1906. Westfield House (now a private house) was a boys' day and boarding classical and mathematical school established in 1842. Even when he was no longer curate, Denning continued to help in the parish, and is remembered for holding regular morning services at the workhouse, afternoon services at Hungerford Newtown, and also managing to fit in services at Denford Park, using a rather old-fashioned bicycle as his means of transport. He was a keen sportsman, and especially good at cricket, as were his brother and two sons. This photograph shows him with his splendid collection of sporting trophies.

The Great Estates Around the Town

24. *above:* **Hungerford Park House, c1920**

Hungerford is surrounded by a small number of large country estates. The land to the east and south belonged to Hungerford Park House, built c1795 in the Italianate style. This photograph shows the garden front, with its croquet lawn and two tennis courts. An earlier house, built by Queen Elizabeth I for her favourite, Robert Devereux, Earl of Essex, stood on this site, and had been the home of the Barons of Hungerford. The house shown in this photograph was demolished in 1960 and only the imposing gates and lodges remind us of its former glory. The estate is now owned by the de Walden family, of Avington Manor.

25. Littlecote House, c1920

To the west of Hungerford is land previously belonging to Littlecote House. This splendid Tudor manor house was a parliamentarian stronghold during the Civil War, and still contains part of a fine collection of Cromwellian armour, much of which was removed to the Royal Armouries Museum at Leeds. In the grounds are remains of an important group of Roman buildings including an Orpheus mosaic. (It is now a hotel owned by Warnerbreaks).

26. Chilton Lodge, 1918

To the north of the town is the estate of Chilton Lodge, now owned by Mr Gerald Ward. In 1663 it was bought by the lawyer, diarist and politician Sir Bulstrode Whitelocke, a distinguished character in the Civil War and Commonwealth period, who died there in 1676. The estate was afterwards sold to John Holwell, one of the sufferers in the 'Black Hole' of Calcutta, and subsequently governor. In 1796 the property was acquired by John Pearse (later MP for Devizes), who demolished the old mansion and built another. During the 19th century, a new Chilton Lodge was built to a design by Sir William Pilkington, comprising a south front and a west front each of five bays the south being particularly handsome incorporating a full-height Corinthian portico, with an east front of seven bays, and with a large north stable court. The kitchen gardens were made famous by the past head gardener, Mr Harry Dodson, whose television series on the Victorian kitchen garden was broadcast by the BBC in 1987.

27. Eddington House, 1903

Standing about one mile north of the village of Eddington, Eddington House owned land to the north and east of Hungerford. The house is in two distinct parts - that to the left (south) is rendered with a stucco cornice and parapet, and dates from the early 1800s, whilst the northern part is a late 19th century addition in red brick. During the early 1900s it was owned by Major ER Portal, one of whose five sons was to become Chief of the Air Staff during the Second World War. Air Chief Marshall Sir Charles Portal, KCB, CB, DSO, MC, Lord Portal of Hungerford, was known locally as 'Peter', and was a keen member of the local cricket club, as were his father and brothers.

28. Inglewood House, 1903

Inglewood lies between Hungerford and Kintbury. The fine mansion shown in this photograph is thought to have been built at the end of the 18th century, with further extensions between 1829 and 1863. On 10 April 1912 there was a major fire in the basement, and the staff rushed to remove valuable works of art to the lawns whilst the fire was extinguished. It was a source of great pride to the local fire brigade that the new Hungerford steam-propelled 'Dreadnought' engine arrived well in advance of the Newbury fire crew, which was still horse-drawn! Inglewood House was sold by the owner Colonel Walmesley in 1928 for use as a Catholic college by the De La Salle brothers. From 1975 it was a health hydro, but it is soon to be developed as a retirement country house and village by Audley Court.

29. Denford House, 1903

The manor of Denford dates from before Domesday, but the house in the photograph was built in 1832 and was designed by Sir Jeffry Wyatville. The owner, George Henry Cherry, was Sheriff of Berkshire in 1829. The house and manor later passed to his two sons, George Charles Cherry (who was Sheriff of Berkshire in 1871), and Major-General Apsley Cherry. On the latter's death in 1907, the estate passed to his own son Apsley Cherry-Garrard, who at the age of 24 years, was one of the youngest members of Captain Scott's famous Antarctic 'Terra Nova' expedition of 1910-1913.

30 and 31. The Hungerford Town Brass and Reed Band, 1912

These two photographs show the Town Band at Denford Park on the occasion of their first concert with new instruments. The then owner of the house, Captain Sawbridge (standing in the formal group in the back row, just to the left of centre), had loaned the finance to purchase the instruments, music and music pouches. In 1953 Denford Park became a junior school for New Hall Chelmsford, run by the Canonesses of the Holy Sepulchre, until Norland Nursery Training College (founded in 1892) bought it in 1967. The Norland College moved to Bath in 2002, and the property is again in private ownership.

32. Freeman's Marsh, 1904

The town is contained on the west by ancient common lands known as Freeman's Marsh, through which runs the River Dun. This enchanting photograph shows a tranquil scene of river and marsh, with the thatched cottages at Strongrove Hill in the distance. Occasionally when studying old postcards, one comes across a gem! The message on one copy of this card includes the text, 'Do you recognise Auntie Amy on this card? She was taken when out sketching'.

33. Marsh View Cottages, c1920

At the end of Marsh Lane, the road leading onto Freeman's Marsh, there was a terrace of cottages running up the slope from the road. These cottages, Marsh View, were demolished in the mid 1970s, and a group of new houses was built on the site.

34. *above:* **The Common Port Down, c1910**

On the high ground to the east of the town is the Common – an unspoilt area of 202 acres used over the years for a wide variety of recreational purposes, including golf and steam fairs! The Common is owned and managed by the Town and Manor of Hungerford, and the Commoners have rights of grazing cattle on the land.

35. *below:* **Down Gate, c1910**

The main entrance to the Common is at the Down gate, where there is a small group of cottages with enviable views across the open ground. Adjacent to the gate is a pub called the Downgate, previously known as the Royal Exchange, and during the 19th century as the Spotted Cow.

36. *above:* **Aeroplane on the Common, 1912**

There are many photographs of early aeroplanes which landed on the Common; they caused great local excitement, and the local photographer, Albert Parsons (see plates 124-126), was clearly very interested. He later joined the Royal Flying Corps. This one is very close to the Down Gate. It is a Bristol Prier two-seater monoplane, one of which was used by No 3 Squadron, RFC in 1912, until grounded by the law on the use of monoplanes in September that year.

37. *below:* **Eddington from the Common, c1929**

This view from the western edge of the Common looks across the railway goods yard and Hungerford East signal box, over the Kennet valley towards Eddington village. St Saviour's church can be seen on the rising ground at the extreme right of the photograph.

38. *above:* **Dun Mill, c1910**

With so much water around the town, it is not surprising that there are many water-mills. Indeed, several mills were mentioned in the Domesday Book of 1086, and there are written records of Dun Mill since 1494. It was a fulling mill during the 17th century, and the present mill dates from the 18th century. When the canal was built immediately adjacent to it, the owners were able to take great advantage of an alternative means of transport to and from the mill. There has been a famous trout farm here since 1907.

39. *below:* **Dun Mill Bridge and Denford Mill, c1920**

The water in the immediate foreground is the Kennet and Avon Canal, and beyond this is the River Dun, with its charming triple-arched bridge downstream of Dun Mill. In the background is Denford Mill (on the river Kennet), a five-bay working mill with the miller's house on its right, now a private house.

40. Denford Mill, 1904

The mill was used during the 19th century as a fulling mill in the cloth industry, for which a copious supply of water was required. In this photograph it can be seen that the mill is still working, many years before being converted for residential use.

41. Eddington Mill, c1911

The manor of Eddington is listed in the Domesday Book with a mill and over 500 acres. The 1844 edition of The Miller states that Eddington Mill was well known throughout the West Country. The mill continued to mill flour until c1952, after which it was used for fertiliser storage until finally closing in 1959.

42. Digging Eddington lake, 1927
Upstream of Eddington Mill is a fine lake. This photograph shows
the work in progress, with Eddington Mill at the far end of the
excavations, on the left.

Beating the Bounds, 8 July 1913

43. A look at the map

Tradition has it that each year the elders of all towns should walk around the town limits, ensuring that the boundary is secure and undisputed. This excursion should involve as many members of the community as possible, both young and old, so that everyone shall come to know the boundary markers, and future generations shall be able to protect the boundary. In 1913 the local photographer, Albert Parsons, followed the Beating of the Bounds, and his very complete photographic record, of which a small selection is included here, provides us with a wonderful insight into a particular day in the life of Hungerford. At various points they stop to consult the map, to ensure that the exact boundary is followed.

44. At Denford Mill

The party takes a rest during the long excursion. This photograph was probably taken at Denford Mill, looking north towards Lower Denford cottages, with Mill Cottage on the right of the photograph.

"BUMPING"

BEATING THE BOUNDS HUNGERFORD 8.7.13

718

45. *above:* **Bumping**

In order to make the exact position of the many boundary posts more memorable to the party, it was customary for one or other of the younger members of the group to be upended at each post, and to have his head (gently) 'bumped' on it. Few youngsters would fail to remember the experience vividly, and they would be able to pass on their local knowledge to future generations.

46. *below:* **Wading through the river**

Many of Hungerford's boundaries lie along one or other of the local rivers, and in order to Beat the Bounds properly, there is no alternative to wading in and struggling onward through waist-high water. It should be noted that this particular expedition took place in July, when the walk through the river would not have been too unpleasant!

Town and Manor – Tutti-Day

47. Constable, Bellman, and Tutti-men, Hocktide 1910

The Constable, Mr Alfred Allright (grocer) is seated, holding the Lucas Horn, dating from 1634. Behind him is the Bellman, Mr Edward Bushnell, and on either side are the two Tutti-men, Mr Frederick Macklin (of the dairy, left) and Mr Robert Cole (of the Town Mill, right), holding their Tutti-poles. It is thought that the Tutti-poles derive from the West Country name for a nose-gay, or bunch of sweet-smelling flowers. No doubt the Tutti-men were glad of their tutties when visiting some of the less sweet-smelling parts of the town in times gone by!

Commanding the Commoners Penny
Hocktide Hungerford 1914

48. Collecting the Commoner's Penny, Hocktide 1914

On the morning of Tutti-Day, the Assistant Bailiff, who is also the Bellman and Town Crier, walks the length of the High Street and Bridge Street, summoning all Commoners to the Hocktide Court. Any Commoner who is unable to attend is liable to be fined one penny, lest he forfeit his rights to grazing and fishing for the year.

49. 'At nine o'clock in the forenoon', Hocktide 1910

The Constable, Mr Alfred Allright, is about to send the Tutti-men (Mr Alfred Macklin on the left, and Mr Robert Cole on the right) to visit all the Commoners' houses in the town. Some of the Commoners can be seen behind him, waiting to attend the Hocktide Court, which starts at nine o'clock.

Both plates 47 and 49 date from Hocktide 1910, and it is interesting to note that plate 47 shows Frederick Macklin as Tutti-man, whilst plate 49 shows his son Alfred. This is the only known occasion when father and son shared the duty of Tutti-man on the same day!

50. *above:* **The Hocktide Court, 1913**

The court sits in the Town Hall, and is chaired by the Constable (Mr John Adnams, corn and seed merchant), with members of the jury and other Commoners around the table. Seated (from left to right) are George Winterbourne (florist), Thomas Walter Alexander (grocer), George Wren (saddler and ironmonger), [unknown], Dr Harry Pike Major (doctor), John Adnams (Constable, corn and seed merchant), Henry Astley (solicitor), William Mapson (watchmaker), [unknown], and Louis Beard (coal merchant). Standing (from left to right) are Edward Gingell (grocer), Ernest Batt (baker), Henry Crossley (Tutti-man), Edward Bushnell (Bellman), John Tyler (draper, Tutti-man), George Hawkes (ironmonger), Johnny Hawkins (confectioner), Alfred Bartholomew (house furnisher), and Stephen Clifford (bootmaker).

51. 'A kiss at the door', Hocktide 1911

It is no longer the duty of the Tutti-men to collect rents and tithes, but other traditions have taken their place, and it is usual to demand a kiss of the lady of the house. The Tutti-men are visiting the Queen Ann house (15/16 High Street), and part of the shop-front of Alfred Allright's shop (earthenware, lino and carpet, shoes, china and glass, drapery) can be seen on the right of the photograph (now owned by Co-op, but shop-front removed).

52. 'A kiss at the window', Hocktide, c1930

Sometimes extreme measures have to be taken by the Tutti-men to succeed in their aim of obtaining a kiss. Here a ladder is required to gain access to the first floor of the Three Swans Hotel. Co-operation and team-effort appear to have won the day!

53. *above:* **At the workhouse, Hocktide 1913**
Although it was not a property attracting Commoner's Rights, it was usual for the Tutti-men to visit the Hungerford and Ramsbury Union workhouse in Park Street during their journey around the town. The photograph shows some of the staff and residents greeting the Tutti-men.

54. *below:* **At the laundry, 1912**
Another establishment frequently photographed on Tutti-day was the Hungerford Laundry in Everlands Road (see also plates 152 and 153). Not surprisingly, the standard of dress here was very high, with all the ladies wearing flowers in their hair.

55. Shoeing the colts, Hocktide 1913

When the business of the Hocktide Court is complete, the
Commoners and their invited guests celebrate Tutti-Day with the
Hocktide Lunch, previously held in the Three Swans Hotel, but
more recently a grander affair in the Corn Exchange. After lunch has
been enjoyed to its full, it is traditional for all newcomers who are
attending lunch for the first time to be required to endure an
initiation ceremony!

Each newcomer, known as a 'colt', is shod by the local blacksmith,
who hammers a horseshoe nail into his foot. The colt is only released
when he shouts the 'magic' word of 'punch', and pays a contribution
to his meal. The blacksmith is seen here hard at work, whilst other
Commoners look on and puff at their clay pipes. The seated
gentleman is holding a bowl containing the 'Plantagenet Punch', still
made to a traditional recipe. It is to be hoped that the man in the
foreground on the left is not the local dentist!

Lower High Street

56. Three Swans Hotel courtyard, c1905
The Three Swans Hotel stands in the very heart of the town, and this photograph of the courtyard shows the clock-tower of the Corn Exchange above the roof line of its High Street frontage. The market-place was an ideal position for a coaching inn. Note the hand cart on the right of the yard. The Three Swans was one of several places where flys could be hired for travelling to neighbouring villages. The driver of the Three Swans' fly was Mr Fishlock.

57. Three Swans Hotel, c1876
This photograph is one of a series of eight splendid Cartes de Visite c1875 by William Softley Parry, who was a toy dealer and photographer in Bridge Street. John Clarke Free had been innkeeper of the Three Swans since c1850 – maybe he is one of those standing in the courtyard archway.
The next building to the left is the draper's shop of Charles Robinson, this being several years before the Capital and Counties Bank redeveloped the site in 1882 (now Lloyds TSB). The adjacent building on the left had been a bank since c1844, when it had opened as a branch of the Wiltshire banking firm of Tanner and Pinckney, later taken over by the London and County Bank c1864 (now NatWest Bank).

58. *above:* **Three Swans Hotel, c1900**

This lantern slide shows a lady and child in a pony and trap waiting outside the Three Swans Hotel. On the door-case (which is in a different position to the modern entrance) is painted Francis Waldron Church, the innkeeper from c1895 until the First World War. On the wall above the entrance is the badge of the Cyclists Touring Club, founded (as the Bicycle Touring Club) in 1878. To the left is part of the Capital and Counties Bank (now Lloyds TSB). Beyond the arch to the Three Swans is the Bell Inn.

59. *below:* **Three grocers in the lower High Street, c1920**

On the left is AJ Killick, grocer (now 'Hungerford Gourmet Oriental Chinese Food Takeaway'). The shop-front is virtually unchanged today. The fine Queen Anne building in the centre of the photograph has already been greatly altered to accommodate the shop-front of the Reading Co-operative Society (now Co-operative Group supermarket), and further down the street is the classic International Stores frontage – making three grocers within about thirty metres!

60. The post office, 14 High Street, c1905

Records of the post office in Hungerford exist from as early as 1695.
The post office was in Charnham Street during the coaching days of
the 18th century, later moving to the High Street. From 1857-c1890
it was at 25 High Street (see plate 141), when it moved to the site
shown in this photograph, 14 High Street (now part of Co-operative
Group supermarket). When telephones were installed in Hungerford
in 1907, this was the site of the first exchange. In 1914 the post office
moved to the newly-built premises on the opposite side of the High
Street. Post Office Counters has been within Martin's, the newsagent,
since 1990.

61. WH Smith, 6 High Street, c1918

The well-known firm of WH Smith & Son had a shop in the High
Street (now part of Martin's, the newsagent) from 1906. Before this,
the premises had been a draper's business since the 18th century,
first in the Lye family and then the Killick family. This photograph
was taken by Templeman of Stoke-on-Trent, who took many wartime photographs in Hungerford.

62. Higgs, 5 High Street, and Hawkes, 3 High Street, c1895
In the centre of the photograph are the premises of Joseph Stuart
Higgs, draper here from c1885 (now Althea's outfitters). Another
member of the family ran Higgs Bros, grocer's, at 122 High Street
from c1885 until c1920. On the right is Samuel Hawkes –
photographer, hairdresser and tobacconist (now the Tutti Pole
Tea Shop).

63. Lower High Street, c1911

This charming photograph gives a general view, in which the buildings
have changed little. There does seem to be an air of tranquillity, though,
due mainly to the lack of motor cars! From the left of the photograph can
be seen Thomas Fruen's china and glass shop (also the undertaker's and
until recently Walton's Clothing), and Faringdon House, Dr Walter
Dickson's home and surgery (now Dunbar's Delicatessen).

64. Hutchins' butcher's shop, 13 High Street, c1920

A fine display of meat is on show outside Hutchins the butchers. Indeed, it is hard to see how one gained access to the shop with the lambs hanging over the doorway! Thomas Hutchins started the butcher's business here c1844, and it was continued by his wife Sarah after his death. From 1906 the business was always referred to as 'Hutchins & Co'. There was a slaughter-house behind the shop. The business was later bought by Mr Edward Pratt, who traded until the 1960s. (It is now Shaw Trust Charity shop, and Framemakers).

65. Bridge House, 20 June 1897

The house is shown specially decorated for Queen Victoria's Diamond Jubilee. There exists a matching photograph (not included) showing the other end of the house decorated with '1897'. Great festivities were arranged in the town to celebrate the Diamond Jubilee, and they were enjoyed to the full during a day of glorious 'Queen's' weather. With church bells, bands, processions, and a church service packed to overflowing, the morning was a continuous succession of festivities. In the afternoon, at three o'clock, a street party was organised in the Croft, with about a thousand adults and children sitting down at a long row of tables in the shade of The Avenue. At half past four, a series of sports on the Downs (the Common) was organised, ending with the Hungerford Grand National Steeplechase, from the Bath Road through the two rivers and the canal at Denford to the winning post on the Downs. The day ended with a torch lit procession through the town and a bonfire and fireworks on the Downs.

The Canal

66. *above:* **The canal, c1906**

The Western Canal was opened from Newbury to Hungerford in 1798 and eventually completed as the Kennet and Avon Canal in 1810. It was cut right through the centre of Hungerford, several houses being demolished to make way. Willow Lodge, the house on the extreme left of the photograph, was built after the canal was completed, in 1826.

67. *below:* **Hungerford wharf, c1900**

A wharf and grading station were established, and considerable trade flourished. Goods included gravel, chalk and whiting for the westerly route, and timber for the east. Grain and flour were carried equally in both directions. The Great Western Railway took over the canal in 1852, and trade declined, although at Hungerford, 3,646 tons were loaded even as late as 1890. This photograph shows two men in a barge at the wharf, with timber and gravel nearby. The crane is clearly visible near the warehouse built of Bath stone.

68. *above:* **The canal swing bridge, 1911**

A peaceful summer scene, with two boys looking at the canal, and a horse waiting patiently by its laden cart. His master can be seen in silhouette in the shadow of the load. The swing bridge was on the lane joining the level crossing at the railway station with the path known as 'Boarden Carriage' which leads to Bridge Street. It has now been replaced with an 'up and over' bridge. Behind the hay-cart can be seen the sewage pump-house, built in 1909.

69. *below:* **Celebrations on the canal, 1910**

This outing on a hot summer's day, with flags and parasols galore, was probably to celebrate the coronation of King George V. In the background can be seen some of the many buildings at Wooldridge's builder's yard. A pair of lock gates can be seen lying on the ground at the right edge of the picture,

70. The Quarter-Mile race, 2 August 1913

One of the main sporting features of the year was the annual swimming sports held at the canal wharf each summer. The popularity of this occasion can be judged from the enormous number of spectators. On the extreme left is Mr Percy Jessett, and wearing the fireman's helmet is the Rev Tom Gray. In the Quarter-Mile race, swimmers dived off the starting board, and swam to the lock and back.

71. The Cigarette race, 2 August 1913

The four contestants are 'lighting up' in readiness for the Cigarette race! At the 'off' each swimmer had to swim to the lock and back whilst keeping a lighted cigarette in his mouth. It sounds an impossible task!

The Railway

72. GWR station, c1892

The railway first reached Hungerford in 1847, when a double track broad gauge line was extended from Newbury as the Berkshire and Hampshire Railway. The original terminus station was opened on 21 December 1847. The line was extended through the town to Seend near Devizes in November 1862, requiring considerable changes to the station, in addition to the three new bridges and embankment through the town. The original GWR broad gauge track was changed to standard gauge in July 1874, but this photograph still shows the track laid on longitudinal sleepers, rather than the more familiar type seen today. This view looking west towards the town shows the station building (on the 'down' platform) before the footbridge was built.

74. Steam railcar at Hungerford c1912

In 1902 new station buildings were built to serve the 'up' platform, these being linked to the main station building by a footbridge. This photograph shows a steam railcar – incorporating engine and carriage in a single unit. The idea was never very successful, probably because of the limited amount of seating available. Note that the track has now been re-laid on standard sleepers (see plate 72).

73. *left:* **Hungerford Station, c1916**

Railway staff are standing on the 'down' platform with a pile of wicker baskets, possibly watercress crates, for which there was a very busy trade from Hungerford. Most of the station buildings were demolished in 1964, and no sign of the original GWR station now remains. The Hungerford West signal box, which can just be seen adjacent to the level crossing at the far end of the 'up' platform, was removed in 1971 after a train derailment had nearly demolished it. (See plates 213-216).

75. GWR bus service, c1910

To improve the service to nearby towns and villages not served by the railway, GWR provided a bus connection service. Shown here is GWR service no. 29, the Marlborough to Hungerford bus, which was routed via Ramsbury. The bus is a 20 hp Milnes Daimler, first registered in Cornwall in August 1905. The Hungerford-Marlborough service started in October 1909, and was extended to a Hungerford-Swindon service in October 1911.

76. Rossmore, Park Street, c1920

Mr Frank Hunt, the station-master, lived at Rossmore, the house on the junction of Station Road and Park Street, until his retirement in 1933. Mr W Neave Chatterton, a local dental surgeon, held a dental surgery at the house, and advertised 'Painless Extractions, Repairs at Shortest Notice, Consultations Free'. At a later date, the house was much altered, with bay windows being added at both ground and first-floor levels, and a two-floor extension to the right-hand side.

The First World War

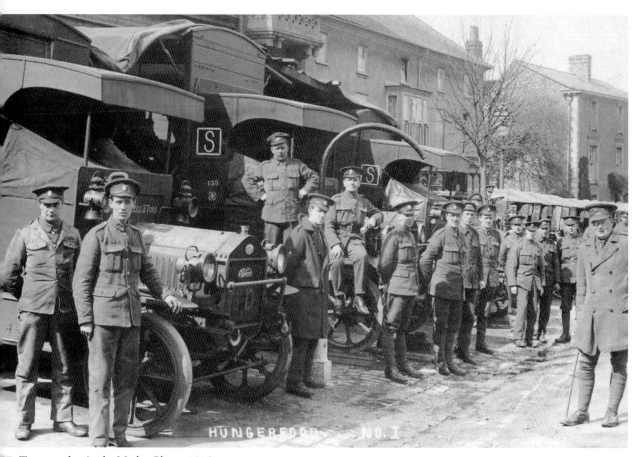

HUNGERFORD · · NO. 1

77. Troops gather in the Market Place, c1915

In January 1915, a newly-formed army unit (180 Company, Royal Army Service Corps, Mechanical Transport) arrived in Hungerford, which was to be its mobilisation station. Initially the unit was small, with one officer and 32 men, with one car, two motor-cycles and 15 lorries! The vehicles were parked in the High Street to start with, and The Croft was used as their parade ground.

78. Troops on the Common, 1915

As the size of the unit grew, the main camp was established on the Common.

79. Off to the Front, 23 July 1915

By July the unit was complete and fully prepared for battle. There were nearly 500 men and 109 vehicles. The whole company assembled in the High Street, and, watched and cheered by the whole town, they set off on their way to Avonmouth, bound for France.

80. The VAD hospital, c1917

In 1914 there was no Ministry of Health and no one had overall control of the hospitals, however the British Red Cross Society, founded in 1870 linked up with the order of St John of Jerusalem in 1909 and formed the organisation known as the Voluntary Aid Detachment or VAD for short. During the War, the old National School building (42 High Street, now Dickins Hopgood Chidley, solicitors) was used as a convalescent hospital, for nursing wounded men who had been sent home from the Front.

81. The hospital kitchen, c1917

The building was refurbished for its new use, with three small wards and a kitchen.

82. The hospital ward, c1917
There were about twenty beds, and most patients were Australians based at Tidworth.

83. *top right:* **Peace celebration dinner, Sunday 6 June 1919**
The Constable, Mr Louis Beard (of the coal yard in Bridge Street – see plate 87), arranged with the vicar, the Rev Tom Gray, a public thanksgiving service for the return of peace. A grand peace celebration dinner was held later in the Corn Exchange.

84. *bottom right:* **The war memorial dedication service, 24 April 1921**
When Hungerford selected a site for its memorial to the 76 men who died in the First World War, it chose well. The previously narrow and congested entrance to the town along Bridge Street (with the International Stores on its east side – see plate 89) was greatly improved by the demolition of the derelict shop and the widening of the road. The triangular strip of land between the two branches of the River Dun was landscaped, and a monument of Dolton stone, with a height of nearly seven metres, was erected. A service of dedication was held on 21 April 1921, attended by a very large crowd. The High Street is seen here nearly full of people. It seems that the entire population of the town must have attended. To obtain enough height for this photograph, Albert Parsons appears to have stood on the bridge parapet – a pretty hazardous position with so many about!

PEACE CELEBRATION DINNER
June 14th 1919

85. Getting as near as possible

Few of those attending could possibly have heard the words spoken by the Rev Tom Gray and the dignitaries taking the service. Many of those standing in Bridge Street, some of whom had brought their bicycles, would just have had to watch in silence. In the background is the Wesleyan chapel in Charnham Street (now Chapel Court).

86. 'In humble gratitude and loving memory'

This 'bird's-eye' view of the service in progress clearly shows the island in Bridge Street on which the old Priory of St John stood in medieval times.

Bridge Street

87. Bridge Street from the canal bridge, 1910

On the extreme right is Beard's coal merchants, started by John Beard in 1832 (now Ad-Hoc Hairdressing Salon). In line with the horse and cart is the barber's shop run by Mr. Francis Batt (now Turpin's Antiques). He also ran the Barley Mow, an inn established c1830, which closed in 1956, (now Stirland's garage). The shop on the left of Bridge Street, with a blind over the pavement, was a confectioner's run by the Phelps family. George Phelps and later his son George Thomas, affectionately known as 'Gingerbread Phelps', ran the bakery, grocery, and confectionary business until the First World War. The shop was subsequently used by Charles Batchelor as a café and confectioner's; Earl's Stores as an ironmonger's; Free's as a furniture shop; and since 1978 by Roxton Sporting Ltd (Fishing and polo equipment, country, leisure and travel clothing). Beyond Mill Cottage (the white-fronted half-hipped building) can be seen the Town Mill (see plate 88).

88. Town Mill, c1900

Opposite the John of Gaunt Inn was the Town Mill, once known as Queen's Mill. We know that there were two water mills in the town in 1275, and one of them was probably on this site. The miller's cottage is on the left of the picture (now Mill Cottage). In the early 1900s the miller was Mr Robert Cole (who later moved to 104 High Street). The mill closed after the First World War and was demolished in 1935, when a private house (Mill Hatch) was built on the site. Beyond the mill can be seen Rumball's butcher's shop. The butcher's business was started c1860 by William Cruse, and Ernest Rumball took over c1896. (Now Furr & Co, Goldsmiths and Jewellers).

89. Bridge Street towards Bear Corner, c1907

Until c1740 the main entrance to the town from the Bath Road had been through a ford across the River Dun, where the railings are on the right edge of this photograph. There were so many complaints about poor access that land was purchased from the Bear Inn, and a new road and two bridges were built to bring the road directly from the Bear across the island on which the Priory of St John had stood some centuries earlier. This is still the line of the present road, and explains why there is such a sharp corner in the middle of Bridge Street near the John of Gaunt Inn. On the left is Freeman Brothers' shop (tobacconists, fishing tackle and fancy goods) who published a number of the photographs used in this book; on the right is the International Stores.

90. International Stores, c1912

This shop was on the east side of Bridge Street, on what is now the
War Memorial Gardens. The shop clearly thrived through the early
years of the 20th century, and a series of similar formal photographs
was taken over several years. After the First World War, however, the
International Stores moved to the High Street, and this site was
cleared for the war memorial in 1920.

91. Bridge Street and war memorial, c1921

After the demolition of the International Stores and the building of the new war memorial,
Bridge Street gained a quite new and spacious feel, providing a far better entrance to the town.

92. Hungerford Printing Works, 2 Bridge Street, 1912

William Franklin, printer, bookseller, auctioneer and registrar of births, marriages and deaths, ran his
business from this shop from c1841 until his death c1865. His widow, Mary, then continued until it
was bought by Alfred New c1881. Mr Ernest Munford came from Huntingdonshire, and was
apprenticed in London before coming to Hungerford in 1912. He continued the printing business
here until c1919, when he moved to 129 High Street. It is interesting that he appears to have
swapped premises at this time with Tom Fruen, the china and glass dealer (also an undertaker),
who moved from 129 High Street down to 2 Bridge Street, where he stayed until 1933.

93. Tanyard Lawn, c1912

This photograph was taken from an upstairs room of Albert Parsons'
Bridge Street studio (see plate 125). The view shows the Bear Hotel
on the left, the Wesleyan chapel in the middle, and on the extreme
right is the splendid Georgian house called Riverside, built c1810
(now Great Grooms Antiques and Fine Paintings). This had been
the site of Hungerford's tannery since at least 1640, and it continued
as such until 1886. The lawn shown in this picture was known as
Tanyard Lawn. The Tanyard chimney was demolished c1908.

94. Bear Corner and Charnham Street, 1903

This view looks west from the Bear Corner: over the front entrance
of the Bear can be seen the name of Edith Osmond, who ran the
inn for only a few years around 1900. The Triumph cycle advert on
the right is on the wall of Stradling's cycle shop (see plate 97).

95. *above:* **Charnham Street, c1906**

A fine summer day has brought many people out in their 'Sunday best'. Perched somewhat precariously on the bicycle is a young child. The text on the postcard includes the comment: 'What do you think of your little Tommy here?'! The Sun Inn was run at this time by Mr Francis Jessett, member of a large Hungerford family.

96. *below:* **Charnham Street, c1919**

On the extreme left is The Hungerford Gas Company showroom (now residential). Beyond it are the premises of John Waller Horne (now Costcutter supermarket), described in *Kelly's Directory* of 1903 and 1911 as 'carman and jobmaster', with horses and traps to let or hire. In 1895 he was at the Plough Inn in the High Street (see plate 127), where he hired 'waggonettes and traps'.

97. WH Giles, Hungerford carrier, c1918

The dozen or so local carriers fulfilled a vital role in the community, providing a link with adjacent towns and villages in the days before any 'public' transport. One Hungerford carrier was William Harry Giles, who provided carriage to Newbury three days a week from 1903. He is photographed here with his sons Harry (standing) and Percy (in the driving seat), and their Daimler coach. The photograph is taken outside the premises of Stradling and Plenty (now Roberta Hair and Beauty) next to the Wesleyan chapel in Charnham Street.

98. Wesleyan chapel, Charnham Street, c1910

The Wesleyan chapel was built in 1869 at a cost of about £3,000. It stood on the site of the White Hart Inn (which traded from 1686 until 1864), opposite the Bear, and therefore occupied a prominent position in the town until it was demolished in 1971. The site is now a residential development called Chapel Court.

99. Charnham Street, 1906

Beyond the cottages on the left (long since demolished) can be seen the Red Lion (now Casanova's restaurant), advertising Finn's Genuine Ales and Stout. In the foreground on the right is one of the crook-shaped water pipes, used to supply water-carts which damped down the dusty roads in dry weather. There were several other water pipes around the town, some of which can be seen in this book; they were installed c1904 and used until the main roads were macadamised. One resident recalls that 'the sound of the watering-cart going up and down the street heralded to us children the start of summer'.

100. Faulknor Square, c1912

This lovely square is seen in this photograph as a splendid grassed
area, screened from the Bath Road by a tall well-trimmed hedge.
Both the south and west terraces seen here were built c1740,
although they have interesting differences in detail.

The Fire Brigade

101. The first steam fire engine, c1908

The original hand-operated fire pump had been kept in the Town Hall during the 19th century, but in 1891 the town acquired its first steam fire pump, a 'Greenwich', made by the firm of Merryweather. The pump was horse-drawn and suffered a number of idiosyncrasies, so it required special skills to operate the engine successfully! These were well mastered by the newly-formed Volunteer Fire Brigade, and on 18 November 1891 a public demonstration of the new Greenwich machine was staged at the Town Hall. Four fine horses hauled the engine at a gallop along the street from the fire station in Charnham Street to the canal wharf. One thousand feet of hose was extended up the street, and within seven and a half minutes, the pump was at full pressure, and able to throw a jet of water 30 or 40 ft over the Town Hall. When tested back at the wharf, it achieved a jet of about 150 ft, and the admiring crowds cheered enthusiastically. To celebrate the event a dinner was held in the Corn Exchange, about one hundred gentlemen being present. This photograph (probably at Denford Mill) shows the Greenwich engine being tested by Mr Alfred Macklin (left) and Mr Harry Champ.

102. The HVFB
at the fire station, c1891

The memoirs of Mr Astley, the local solicitor, include 'Another event of note was the start of the Hungerford Voluntary Fire Brigade in 1891. Previously there was no brigade. There were four of us, George Cottrell, owner of the Iron Works at Eddington; George Platt, the brewer; myself, and John Beard, the coal merchant. I must confess I thought we were aiming rather high when we decided to go in for a 'steamer'. However, our project was well supported by the residents of the town and neighbourhood and we soon had sufficient money to purchase the engine and equip the brigade. You can imagine how proud we all felt when we first appeared in our new uniforms and shining brass helmets!'. To accommodate the new Greenwich fire engine, the town's first fire station was built in Charnham Street, adjacent to Faulknor Square. On the left is Mr George Platt (who gave the premises adjacent to the tannery for use as a fire station); George Cottrell (the Captain of the Brigade); the branchmen were Messrs Beard, Hoskings, Alexander and Jessett; the firemen were Messrs Astley, Cundell, Adnams and Killick; chief engineer was Mr W Sperring, and his assistant was Mr Dear.

103. The Dreadnought fire engine, 1910

Good though the Greenwich fire engine had been, technology was rapidly advancing, and the need for a self-propelled machine was evident. In 1910 the town took possession of a new and more powerful Merryweather steam fire engine, named 'The Dreadnought'. This photograph shows the scene at the fire station on the hand-over day. The driver is Mr Harper of Merryweather's, but the entire brigade has managed to climb aboard. Mr George Cottrell (the Captain of the Brigade) is sitting on the driver's left, and the Rev Tom Gray is on his right. Note the lights, the fire-bell and the solid tyres.

104. Preparing for the grand demonstration, 1910

On 23 September 1910 the new engine was christened outside the Town Hall. The entire town seemed to be there for the occasion. Miss Sawbridge, daughter of Captain Sawbridge of Denford Park, who had been one of the main contributors towards its purchase, lifted a bottle of champagne, and, at the third attempt, smashed it against the engine, naming it 'The Dreadnought'.

The engine went up the High Street to the top of Salisbury Road before returning to the wharf, where, remembering the fine demonstration put on in 1891 when the previous engine had been delivered, the fire brigade arranged a similar demonstration at the wharf, again attended by a large crowd of town officials and the general public. Final preparations are well in hand; the inlet hose is already in the canal.

105. Demonstrating The Dreadnought, 1910

'The Power of the Pump was Marvellous to Behold!' The town was justifiably proud of its new acquisition, and the wharf, with a ready supply of water, proved to be a perfect arena for the very large crowd who gathered. The engine could travel at speeds of 30 mph, deliver 300 gallons of water per minute, and send a jet of water 150 ft into the air. Several of the wharf buildings can be seen in the background.

106. Funeral of Mr FR Pratt, 9 June 1910

Two months before the new fire engine came to Hungerford, one of
the brigade members, Mr FR Pratt, landlord of the Bear Hotel, was
killed in a road traffic accident. A grand funeral was arranged, with
his colleagues in the fire brigade pulling the funeral carriage from
the Bear along Charnham Street to St Saviour's church in
Eddington. This photograph shows the funeral procession passing
Faulknor Square. On the left is Alec Townsin's refreshment rooms
(now Bow House antiques and gifts) in Faulknor Square, then the
fire station (now The Finishing Touch gifts), with the Bear Hotel in
the distance. On the right is James Stradling's cycle shop, a business
founded in Newbury in 1877 (now Sapphire Furnishings), and the
Red Lion Inn (now Casanova's restaurant).

Eddington

107. Eddington from Eddington Bridge, 1915
A bridge over the Kennet at Hungerford was mentioned as long ago as 1275. Lying on the north bank of the River Kennet, Eddington was a self-contained village, with its own post office, shops, church, garage, inn, infant school and ironworks providing plenty of local employment.

108. Oxford Street, Eddington, c1911

Taken from the main road looking north towards Linden Cottage, this photograph shows the Eddington post office on the right (now a private house), opposite which is a terrace of cottages with interesting decorative brickwork (demolished 1966 before the building of Kennet Court). Beyond the post office is one of Hungerford's very early garages, with the name Hillsdon & Co, Eddington Motor Works, previously the Infant National School from 1869 (6 Oxford Street, now a private house). Mr CO Hillsdon lived next door at Buckland House.

109. Eddington post office, c1907

Trade directories as far back as 1844 mention the Jessett family grocery shop in Eddington. The business passed from Francis to George to Mrs Jane Jessett, and c1891 to Mr Frederick Jessett, whose shop it was at the time of this photograph. The family lived in the house, behind which was the large bakery. Other members of this large family owned shops in other parts of Hungerford.

For example, in *Kelly's* of 1920 we find Francis Jessett, the Sun public house, Charnham Street; Frederick Jessett, baker, Charnham Street; and Thomas Jessett, beer retailer, Park Street. The Victorian post-box in the wall of the building is still in use today. On the left can be seen Mr Lewington's coal cart on its rounds.

110. Jessett's bakery, 1915

During the First World War, Frederick Jessett supplied bread to the troops stationed at Hungerford (see plates 77-79). The photograph shows many dozen loaves of various shapes and sizes, ready to be delivered to the army.

111. Supplying bread to the troops, 1915

It seems that the regular deliveries of bread to the army on the Common were made by commissioning a furniture wagon. An officer can be seen checking the delivery against his order form.

112. Oxford Street, Eddington, c1912

The grocery shop on the right was run by two Misses Winkworth, and although now a private house, the 'shop' window and doorway are little changed today. On the left is a group of workers at the wheelwright and blacksmith, including Norman Higgins (blacksmith), Jim Middleton (carpenter) and Bill Wiggins (blacksmith). At the far end of this part of Oxford Street is Linden Cottage, where the road turns left towards Eddington Bridge.

113. Folly Hill, c1908

The buildings are little different today, with Hansel's Cottage on the left and St Saviour's church
partly hidden by The Hermitage on the right. The road was widened at this point during the 1970s
to accommodate the heavy use made of this trunk road.

114. St Saviour's church, Eddington, c1920

This church was built 'for the convenience of the northern part of the parish' and opened in 1868. The land was given by William
Honywood of Chilton Lodge, and the church was built by the local firm of Thomas Wooldridge at a cost of £2,000. It is in Early
English style and was designed by Sir Arthur Blomfield. Standing on high ground overlooking the Kennet valley and the town of
Hungerford, the churchyard to the north of the church is still used today as the parish burial ground.

115. St Saviour's church, c1920

The church seated 250 people, and was in regular use for nearly 100 years until it closed c1956. It was converted into a private house (Church House) in 1977.

116. Eddington turnpike gate, c1850

The Eddington turnpike is thought to have been on Folly Hill, the road north from Eddington towards Shefford and Wantage, and the gate was possibly at the junction with the Upper Eddington Road, opposite the gate to St Saviour's church (now Church House). If the gatekeeper lived in the tiny cottage with his family, then it must indeed have been crowded, as there are at least nine people in the photograph!

117. Cottrell, Rose & Co Ltd, 1903

There were two large iron foundries in Hungerford at the start of the 20th century. One of these was George Cottrell's Iron Works in Eddington, established c1869. Their entry in *Kelly's Directory* describes them as 'iron founders, millwrights, agricultural implement and boiler makers, patentees of the 'Climax' (gold medal) folding elevator and prize medal engines and water carts'. The firm closed c1911 and few of the original buildings remain now.

IMPROVED FARM CART.

This Cart is well adapted for all farm and general purposes, the body being roomy and strongly framed together of well-seasoned English timber, and fitted with improved tipping arrangement.

PRICES.

	£	s.	d.
Strong One Horse Cart, with 4in. wheels	15	0	0
Head and Tail Ladders, extra	1	10	0

LONDON PATTERN HAY CART

A useful and roomy Cart, with oak frame, plank sides, fitted with tipping apparatus, wheels 5ft. high, with hay ladder over horse, and projecting ladder at back.

Price £19 0 0

Designs upon Application.

Illustrated General Catalogues sent free on application to

COTTRELL, ROSE & Co., Ltd.,

EDDINGTON IRON AND WAGON WORKS,

HUNGERFORD,

BERKS., ENGLAND.

118. Cottrell, Rose & Co, catalogue, 1897
The goods on offer seem to be remarkable value for money, with the Improved One Horse Cart selling for £15 0s 0d and the award winning 'Climax' Elevator just £49 10s 0d.

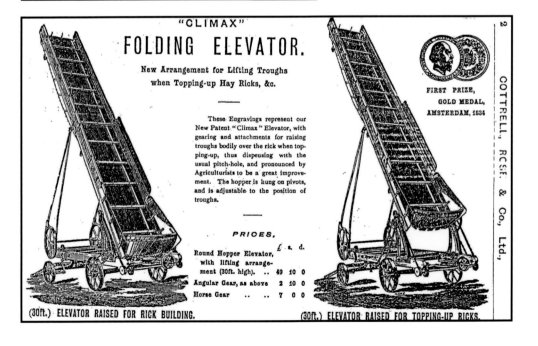

"CLIMAX"
FOLDING ELEVATOR.

New Arrangement for Lifting Troughs when Topping-up Hay Ricks, &c.

These Engravings represent our New Patent "Climax" Elevator, with gearing and attachments for raising troughs bodily over the rick when topping-up, thus dispensing with the usual pitch-hole, and pronounced by Agriculturists to be a great improvement. The hopper is hung on pivots, and is adjustable to the position of troughs.

PRICES.

	£	s.	d.
Round Hopper Elevator, with lifting arrangement (30ft. high)..	49	10	0
Angular Gear, as above	2	10	0
Horse Gear ..	7	0	0

FIRST PRIZE, GOLD MEDAL, AMSTERDAM, 1834.

COTTRELL, ROSE & Co., Ltd.,

(30ft.) ELEVATOR RAISED FOR RICK BUILDING.

(30ft.) ELEVATOR RAISED FOR TOPPING-UP RICKS.

119. *above:* **Eddington Garage, c1922**

After Cottrell's Iron Works closed, the site was used as a motor business, initially called Eddington Garage. In 1922 it was bought by Bill Norman, and the business ran under the name of Norman's Garage until 1970. This photograph is taken looking north across the forecourt. (It is now the Total petrol station).

120. *right:* **Henry Gibbons and Son, catalogue, c1895**

Not to be outdone by Cottrell's their competitors, the other local engineering firm of Henry Gibbons & Son, of the Kennet Works in Charnham Street (now the Somerfield Texaco petrol station) advertised themselves as 'manufacturer of Gibbons' patent moulding machines, lawn mower sharpeners, patent safety flush bolts and manufacturers of steam and hot water fittings and all kinds of agricultural implements (medals awarded)'. This firm had been established by Richard Gibbons at Ramsbury in 1814. He moved to 16 Bridge Street, Hungerford, in 1824 before building a new foundry in Charnham Street in 1839.

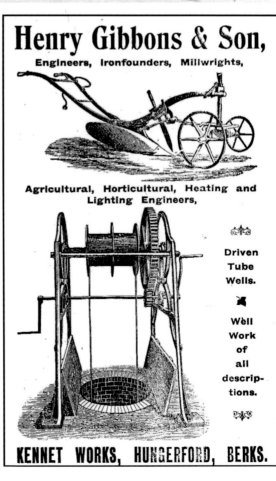

Henry Gibbons & Son,

Engineers, Ironfounders, Millwrights,

Agricultural, Horticultural, Heating and Lighting Engineers,

Driven Tube Wells.

Well Work of all descriptions.

KENNET WORKS, HUNGERFORD, BERKS.

121. Kennet Motor Works. c1939

Henry Gibbons Engineering Works closed in 1931, the site being
taken over as the Kennet Motor Works in 1936 by Mr Ludford.
The business was quite a large one for the period, with five petrol
pumps on the forecourt. In the photograph are the Maxwell
breakdown truck, an Austin Seven and an Austin Ten. The pump
price of Cleveland petrol was 1s 7d per gallon. It is now the
Somerfield Texaco petrol station.

Portraits

122. Edward Bushnell, Bellman, 1920

Mr Edward Bushnell was Town Crier from 1880 until 1923. He ran a coffee tavern in the High Street (now the Tutti Pole Restaurant), and was responsible for the running of the Town Hall and Corn Exchange. Amongst many other duties he was responsible for ringing the fire bell on the roof of the Town Hall in the event of a fire, for which he was paid 5s 0d – a considerable sum at the time. He was succeeded in his role of Bellman and Town Crier by his son Sidney Bushnell, and later by the present Bellman, Robin Tubb, who is Edward Bushnell's great-grandson. The office of Bellman has therefore been held by the same family in Hungerford for well over a century, and the town celebrated Robin's 50 years as Bellman and Town Crier on 2 June 2007.

123. Tom Gray, c1920

The Reverend William Edward Thomas
Seccombe Gray was always known as
Tom. He was vicar of Hungerford from
1909 until 1924, and was much involved
in the community life of the town during
the years covered by many of the
photographs in this book. He was a very
popular man and a keen sportsman,
fishing and shooting being his special
interests. Indeed he wrote a book on
fishing under the pen-name 'Silver
Devon' entitled *Leaves from an Angler's
Notebook*. He was an active member of
the Hungerford Volunteer Fire Brigade,
rising to the most senior rank of captain,
and skilfully managed to combine his
'dog-collar' with his fireman's uniform!

Albert Parsons

124. Albert Parsons, c1914

A large number of the photographs in this book were taken by
one photographer, Albert Parsons, who came to Hungerford in
c1902. The quality of his work is second to none, and his output
was prolific. He is shown here as proud owner of his 1908 Rover
6 hp car, which was produced in dark green paintwork, with dark
red upholstery, and capable of speeds of up to 50 mph! The
vehicle was fitted with two brake pedals, whilst speed was
controlled by hand rather than by a foot pedal.

125. Bridge Street, c1914
Initially, Mr Parsons was unable to find ideal premises for a photographic studio, so he and his wife made their first home in Church Street, and built a studio in the garden. Within a few years, however, he was able to move to a prime site at 1 Bridge Street, next to the Hungerford Printing Works.

126. Upper High Street, c1918
Albert Parsons joined the Royal Flying Corps during the war, and soon after his return home the family moved to 30 High Street (now Barclays Bank), premises previously owned by William Mapson, a watch-maker and photographer who had worked there since 1891. He later expanded his business to include car hire. The photograph shows the studio on the extreme right, with his car standing outside. When Albert Parsons died in 1950, the business closed, and the property was used as the Gateway Café (run by Miss Catherine Rose) until being redeveloped by Barclays Bank, which opened in 1967.

127. The Plough Inn, 49 High Street, c1910
There were three inns near the top of the High Street: the Salisbury
Arms (now a private house), the Borough Arms
(as now), and the Plough. The Plough dated from c1854,
and closed around the First World War (now residential).

128. *above:* **Upper High Street, 1915**
The horse and cart in the distance are collecting water from the pump at Atherton field, later Atherton Crescent. On the left are the cottages which were later demolished to make way for the High Street flats called Fairfields. Note that 55-57 High Street (on the right) were thatched cottages at the time.

129. *below:* **Salisbury Road, c1910**
Moving now to the southern limits of the town, this photograph shows the view looking back towards the town. On the left is Church Way, and with very few buildings to block the view, the new Council School (built 1910) is clearly visible on the high ground of Fairview Road. Just visible down the hill is the St John's mission hall (see plate 130).

130. Interior of St John's mission hall, c1910

The mission hall (see also plates 186 and 187) was built in 1899, funded by Lady Pearce (of Chilton Lodge). It was run by the Church Army, and was under the care of Captain Birt (and from 1920 by Captain Robert Manfield and his sister). In addition to the regular services, 'Band of Cheer' sessions were held every Wednesday afternoon, when a bun and cup of tea cost 1d. The hall was also used on numerous occasions for whist drives, concerts, and other activities. This photograph was clearly taken at Harvest Thanksgiving, and the man on the right of the photograph is thought to be Captain Birt, shown with his family.

131. Gathering barley in Atherton field, 1909

This splendid photograph shows the Macklin family and helpers
harvesting - six acres of barley produced 88 sacks. The field had
earlier belonged to Lady Atherton, who is said to have offered the
field to the town as a cemetery. This plan was not followed through,
however, and Atherton Crescent, a fine curved line of houses set well
back from the main road, was built in 1921.

132. Upper High Street, c1905
The steam traction engine stands outside the Salisbury Arms which traded from c1850 until after the First World War. The High Street narrows at this point, which represents the southern limit of the town before the 19th century. There was a boundary gate across the road here until the early 19th century.

133. Upper High Street, 1911
The lady on the left is standing in the doorway of Alfred Mills, butcher's (now residential). The next shop was Ernest W Batt, bakery and cake shop (now Orwell House).

134. WH Giles, 43 High Street, c1908

William Harry Giles, the Hungerford carrier, lived and worked from
43 High Street, adjacent to the National School. His younger son
Percy is shown here holding the horse, and sitting on the cart are his
elder son Harry (holding the whip) and Bob Newhook.

135. Macklin's Dairy, 89 High Street, c1905

Mr Frederick Macklin is seen here sitting in his wagonette outside
his dairy in the High Street (now residential). The driver is his son
Alfred Macklin. On the driver's seat support is the Hungerford crest
and the name 'Eclipse'. Mr Macklin used to lead the cows from the
Common down Cow Lane (Park Street) and up the High Street to
the dairy for milking.

136. Upper High Street, 1911

The bicycle on the left is leaning against William Harris' baker's and grocer's shop. The business had started in the 19th century and closed in 1956. Behind the brick wall to the right of the bakery was a blacksmith's yard (now the Launderama).

137. Clifford's, 110 High Street, c1928

The shop sign says that Clifford's boot and shoe business was established in 1700. Records show that in 1869 Stephen Clifford ran a boot and shoemaking business in Charnham Street, and that it moved to 110 High Street (until recently Lane Fox, estate agents, and Marc Allen, estate agents) c1891. The shopkeeper in this photograph is Stephen's son, William Martin Clifford, who ran the business from c1920 until it closed in 1966. Advertisements in the window include Wren's polish, Blanco, Brook's Dye Works in Bristol, K Shoes and Boots, and Comac Shoes.

138. Adnams' corn merchants, 28 High Street, 1912

John Corderoy Adnams ran a seed and corn merchant business from this property from 1873. He lived in the main part of the house, with the shop on the right-hand side. The building is shown decorated for the King's visit of 1912 (see plates 156-170). In 1960 the local solicitors' firm of Charles Lucas and Marshall moved here from Bridge Villa (see plate 65), and the shop front was removed. Adnams' barn was set back behind this building, and part of it is now converted to flats known as The Granary.

139. Market Place, c1876

This photograph is one of a series of Cartes de Visite of Hungerford by W S Parry of Bridge Street (see also plate 57), and shows an important group of buildings in the Market Place. From left to right can be seen Thomas Alexander's grocer's shop (and his house), the post office, Henry Wren's ironmonger's and saddler's, Keen's brewery and the Town Hall.

140. Alexander's stores, 27 High Street, c1912

This timber-framed building is one of the oldest in Hungerford, showing its original frontage without a Georgian 'make-over'. It was Alexander's grocery business for about 128 years. Benjamin Alexander started as a grocer and tea-dealer here in 1844, Thomas Alexander was grocer and wine merchant in 1871, before his son Thomas Walter Alexander followed in 1896. Alexander's was taken over by Norman and Dudley James in 1947, until it eventually closed in 1972. The Hungerford Antiques Arcade opened in 1974. Other members of the Alexander family were ironmongers, farmers, and coal merchants in the area.

141. London & Provincial stores, 25 High Street, c1900

Alexander's heavy coal wagon, with Bill Lewington holding the reins, is standing outside the London & Provincial stores (now Wine Rack). The building has a long and interesting history, having been owned by (amongst others) a doctor and a bishop before becoming a draper's shop. In c1857 it was Hungerford's post office, when Charles Osmond was postmaster. Around 1900 it began a long period as a food shop, first as London & Provincial stores, then in 1902 as Edward Gingell's family grocers, before being bought by Philip Spackman in 1949. Spackman's closed in 1990, since when it has been a wine merchant (currently Wine Rack).

142. Wren's ironmonger and saddler, 24 High Street, c1891

This timber-framed building overlooking the Market Place was the Greyhound Inn in the 18th century. William Alexander opened a saddler's business in part of the building in 1813, and in 1865 Henry Wren and John Matthews expanded it to include ironmongery. Henry Wren died in 1890, and his brother George Wren inherited the property. This photograph was probably taken soon after the change of ownership. On the left are (from left to right) Frederick Rosier (saddler) and George Wren (owner); in the middle are the tinsmith, Mr Tidbury (an apprentice saddler), and in the apron

Mr Gregory (a saddler). On the right are two (unknown) saddlers. The window displays illustrate the extensive range of hardware goods for sale, and on the pavement are garden tools and a variety of harness, saddles, and leather bags. There is a lady standing at the right-hand front window. Perhaps she is George Wren's wife. The ironmonger's continued through the 20th century first as Nicol's (1919-1971) then Paul Good's (1971-1985). It is now Azuza's coffee shop, The Hungerford Bookshop, and The Courtyard.

143. The Market Place, c1895

This early view of the Market Place shows (from left to right): George Wren's ironmonger's and saddler's, Elisha Love's Crown Brewery, the Town Hall and Corn Exchange, Frederick Barnard's fishmongers, and Richard Killick's chemist and drug store. Note the old front on the Crown Brewery, and just two shop fronts on the shops to the right of the Corn Exchange.

144. The Market Place, 1902

There are interesting changes from the previous photograph: by 1902 the Crown Brewery had been re-roofed and re-fronted in mock-Tudor style, and the shops to the right of the Corn Exchange had been refitted with a new three-bay shop front, now housing (from left to right): Frederick Barnard, fishmonger, greengrocer and fruiterer; Annie Barnard, stationers and tobacconist, and Ernest Barnard, house furnishing. The Barnard family lived at Rossmore, Park Street.

145. Barnard's stationers, 21 High Street, c1925

Some years later again, the middle of the three shops was now Ernest Barnard's newsagent, stationery, fancy goods and tobacconist shop, and Alfred Bartholomew was running the antiques shop and cabinet makers on the right. Note the fine pair of gas lamps hanging outside. Adverts include Slazenger rackets and balls, Maharaja cigars, and the *Newbury Weekly News* which was reporting the Town Council elections. (It is now Rayners opticians).

Schools

146. Council School, 1910

In September 1910 a fine new all-age school was built in Fairview Road, replacing the National School (in the High Street) and the Wesleyan school (in Church Street). This photograph was taken from Atherton Hill, looking over the roof tops of Salisbury Row. The main building was for children aged six to fourteen years, and the smaller building on the left was for infants, aged three to five years. The design incorporated the most modern features of its time, including central heating, running water and flush toilets – facilities which were not yet available in many private houses in the town.

147. Nature pond, c1920

The children were encouraged to study nature, and they built a small pond in the school grounds so that they could keep some of the plants and animals gathered from the countryside. Some buildings in Fairview Road can be seen in the background. The teacher in this photograph is Miss Waddington.

148. Boys' gardening class, c1925

In a thoroughly practical way, the curriculum included gardening classes for boys. Note the town crest proudly displayed on the roof of the shed.

149. Mr Camburn's retirement, 1921

The first headmaster of the new Council School was Mr Caleb Camburn. He had previously been headmaster of the Wesleyan school in Church Street from 1886. Under his portrait can be seen the school initials (HCS – Hungerford Council School), the Hungerford town crest (star and crescent), the school motto (devised by Mr Camburn) 'No Quest, No Conquest', and the old county badge of Royal Berkshire depicting a stag under a tree. Behind the group of children can be seen the newly-built houses in Atherton Crescent, and a pair of cottages in Church Way.

The Police

150. The police station, c1910
The police station in Park Street was built in 1864, and is still used
today. Although the interior has been much altered, the external
appearance of the building itself is virtually unchanged.

151. The police reserve, 1919

There are no fewer than 33 men in this photograph, nearly all of them with a moustache, and one of them, the Rev Denning, with a 'dog-collar'. The formal group photograph was taken at the entrance to the police station. Note the roses and ivy on the walls, and the geraniums and clipped box hedges in the gardens.

The Laundry

152. Hungerford laundry, c1910

The Hungerford Sanitary Laundry Co Ltd was established c1908, and took over the large brewery building in Everland Road. The latest equipment was installed, and the firm enjoyed a reputation for the high quality of its work. A report on a visit to the laundry states: 'After inspecting this establishment, I can honestly certify that from the receiving room to the despatch room every detail has been carefully studied, and no expense has been spared to make it a thoroughly up-to-date sanitary laundry, and the motto of the company has been carried out to the letter, viz: Cleanliness, Efficiency, and Sanitation'. The price list includes ladies bodice (3d); silk stockings (3d); doyley (1¼d); ladies' knickers (3½d to 6d); whilst maids' knickers were only 2½d! This photograph shows the ironing room of the laundry and gives some idea of the large scale of the operation.

153. Hungerford laundry delivery team, c1910

A large team of men and horses was required to collect and deliver laundry around the area. Some of them are pictured here in the stable yard. The laundry closed in December 1966 after several changes of ownership, having been renamed The Rose of Hungerford Laundry in the 1950s. Somerfield supermarket and car park was built on the site in 1999.

Church Street

154. Church Street, 1915
This scene at the corner of Croft Road has changed little, apart from
the absence nowadays of iron railings.

155. James' Great Western Mill, c1930

The family milling business of James & Co was a large employer in
the town. Ernest Frank James came to the area as manager at the
Country Flour Mill in Chilton Foliat, and later also ran Denford
Mill. At the end of the First World War they took over part of the
old brewery in Everland Road as a feed mill. More space and more
power were required by the end of the 1920s, and having bought
Kennet House, 19 High Street and its large garden, he proceeded to
build a large new modern mill facing Church Street. This Great
Western Mill opened in 1932. In June 1960, however, the mill
caught fire, and overnight the building was totally destroyed.
(See plates 201 and 202).

King's Visit, 21-26 October 1912

156. Station-master and GWR staff

In October 1912 King George V visited Sir John Ward at Chilton Lodge. The proposed visit captured the enthusiasm of the whole town, which set about the task of preparing and decorating the town with enormous energy. Albert Parsons took the opportunity to photograph every part of the town, and as a result we now have a very full record of a day in the life of Hungerford. This photograph shows Mr Frank Hunt, the station-master of the GWR station, with his staff (no fewer than 26 men at the time).

157. The Constable and feoffees

The town officials were all on parade to welcome His Majesty, and are photographed here at the railway station awaiting his arrival. They include (from left to right) Edward Bushnell (Town Crier), Francis Church (landlord of the Three Swans Hotel), Thomas Freeman (tobacconist), George Platt (brewer), Thomas Alexander, Henry Astley, John Adnams (Constable, corn and seed merchant), George Wren, Alfred Allright, Thomas Walter Alexander (grocer), Louis Beard (coal merchant, in Burberry coat), William Mapson (watchmaker), and (on the extreme right) Frank Hunt (station-master).

158. The King on his way to the station

The day of the King's departure from Hungerford was spoiled by heavy rain. Despite this, the band (on the left) played on, and a large crowd came to cheer. Sadly the profusion of umbrellas must have reduced the view considerably. The King's journey to Hungerford had been non-stop from Paddington, and took one hour and ten minutes, arriving at 7.15pm. He left at 10.40am on Saturday 26 October.

159. The Market Place

Bunting and flags were everywhere, with every shop festooned. Note the very tall telegraph poles, carrying the wires high above the railway bridge.

160. The lower High Street
From left to right can be seen Allright's Universal Stores, the post office and Hutchins & Co butchers.

HUNGERFORD DURING THE KING'S VISIT. 21.10.12

161. Manor House and the lower High Street
On the right of this photograph is the Manor House, where Dr Blake James lived and held his surgery. This was to be the doctors' surgery until 1959 when a new surgery was built in The Croft. Manor House was demolished in 1965 to make way for a petrol filling station (until recently African Trackwoods and the entrance to Somerfield car-park). To the left of Manor House can be seen Arthur Higgs' grocer's shop (now Inklings gift shop and a vacant shop); John Tyler's draper's and milliner's shop (now Three Cooks bakery); Arthur Bingham's chemist shop (now Boots the Chemist); and Earle's ironmonger's store (now the post office building). (See also plates 206-208)

162. The triumphal arch and canal bridge

The sign to the left of the bridge, near the two children, advertises 'Umbrellas Made, Recovered, and Repaired'.

163. *left:* **The canal bridge**

Note the gas lamps on the bridge, and the patriotic welcome 'God Bless You and Yours'.

164. *below:* **The triumphal arch and lower High Street**

Preparations are still in hand, with ladders in place against the triumphal arch.

165. Bridge Street

On the left is the entrance to the canal wharf. The wharf had been run by Thomas Wooldridge, and later by his son John Holmes Wooldridge. In addition to the trade on the canal, they also ran a builder's business here, and were widely acclaimed especially for their work in church restoration. The family lived at 13 Bridge Street (now residential and MJM Antiques) and the builder's business continued to operate until 1967. The redevelopment of the wharf and Canal Walk took place in 1973.

166. Bridge Street and International Stores

On the right is the International Stores. Note how it narrowed the road at this point.

167. Bridge Street from Bear Corner

The River Dun in Bridge Street marked the county boundary between Wiltshire and Berkshire until the boundary changes of 1894. The banner reminds us of this with the message 'Welcome to the Royal County'.

168. Agricultural arch by the Sun Inn

Perhaps the finest decoration of all was the magnificent agricultural arch, built adjacent to the Sun Inn in Charnham Street. H Gibbons and Son now describe themselves on the advertising board as 'General Engineers', but their agricultural origins are evident from the arch. It contains examples of their craft, including scythes, ploughs and harrows, all artistically combined on two of their famous grain elevators.

THE KINGS VISIT TO HUNGERFORD 21.10.12
AGRICULTURAL ARCH

169. *above:* **Agricultural arch with staff of Gibbons' ironworks**

It was a splendid example, and the staff of Gibbons were understandably proud of their achievement, happily posing for a formal photograph under their arch.

170. *below:* **The Bear Corner**

This final photograph of the first edition brings us full circle, showing the scene at the Bear Corner. Note the AA man standing near the signpost. The Bear advertises itself as a 'family hotel' with 'spacious garage'. The age of the car had begun in Hungerford!

After 1930

171. Charlie May's cycle shop, Charnham Street, c1935

The First World War delayed many aspects of social change, including car ownership. As this photograph shows, cycling was still a very important mode of transport in the mid 1930s, twenty years after the previous photograph. Earlier plates in this book illustrate how well retailers showed off their wares in the early years of the 20th century; good displays brought good business, and here we can see that in 1935 Charlie and Eddie May mean business! Charlie May took over the cycle shop from Stradling's (see plate 106). (It is now Sapphire Furnishings).

172 & 173. *below:* **Floods in Charnham Street, 16 May 1932**

Lying as it does in the valleys of both the rivers Kennet and Dun, flooding used to be a frequent event until the middle of the 20th century. Families got used to 'pumping-out' their premises and homes. One well-recorded flood was on 16 May 1932, when Charnham Street was under several inches of water. (*Left*) A car is seen here splashing its way past the Red Lion Inn (now Casanova's restaurant). (Right) The Bear Hotel yard was knee-deep.

174 & 175. Hungerford Carnival in the 1930s

The annual summer carnival was a popular and well-supported event in the town's calendar between the wars. The photograph above (c1934) shows the Constable, Dr Starkey-Smith crowning the Carnival Queen Madge Pine outside the Town Hall and Corn Exchange. The size of the crowd, and the expressions on their faces shows just how seriously the event was taken at this time.

The Carnival procession in 1937 is marching up the High Street past International Stores (now Co-op). Leading the parade is the Bellman and Town Crier, Sid Bushnell, followed by the young heralds Margaret Cox (later Margaret Williams) and Mary McCarthy. The Carnival Queen is Mrs Harvey, with the Constable 'Jimmie' Munford taking her arm. Holding her train are Cissie Clements and Joyce Elliot. The Carnival Queen was always the person who had sold the most raffle tickets! Competition was stiff! There were many celebrations around this time – grand celebrations for the Silver Jubilee of King George V on 6 May 1935, and for the Coronation of King George VI on 12 May 1937. Hungerford knew how to party! Sadly, the Second World War was soon to have a great effect on the whole nation.

176. Edwards' Golden Gallopers, Oct 1950

Both before and after the Second World War the well known Swindon showman, Robert Edwards, who always claimed to have been born in Hungerford High Street, regularly brought his gallopers to Hungerford and other local towns. His first roundabout had been bought second-hand in 1916 for eighty sovereigns! When this photograph from 1950 was taken they had brought 'Chariot Racer', 'Arcade', 'Joy Cars' as well as 'Shooter' and other supporting side stalls. They were a great attraction, nearly filling the High Street.

177. Stop me and Buy One, 1938

Bill Watts is seen here with his T Wall & Sons Ltd 'Stop me and Buy One' tricycle. The photograph is taken in the market place, where Edwards' 'Monte Carlo Rally' ride was erected for the fair. You can just see that the front of the ride is over the white line – a necessity because the ride had to be built around the lime tree. It must have been the only fairground ride in the country with a tree growing out of the centre!

MORALE
HOW TO PLAY YOUR PART

Forget yourself in helping your neighbours. In days of tension this casts out your own fears and worries. Help them to carry out all instructions about air-raids, evacuation, rationing and waste.

Keep the moral standards of the nation high. Don't weaken the home front by trying to wangle something for yourself on the quiet. Make a break with all the personal indulgence, selfishness and private wars which undermine national morale and unity. Everybody has his part to play in the moral re-armament of the nation.

Be a rumour-stopper. Those who love their country sacrifice the luxury of being the ones to pass on the "news." Any patriot shoots a rumour dead on sight. Face the facts, but don't exaggerate them. Prepare to meet them instead. Faith, confidence and cheerfulness are as contagious as fear, depression and grumbling.

The secret of steadiness and inner strength is to listen to God and do what He says. God speaks directly to the heart of every man and woman who is prepared to listen and obey. Write down the thoughts He gives you. His voice can be heard wherever you are—in the home, in the factory, in the air-raid shelter, in the first-aid post.

Forearm yourself by listening to God first thing every morning. This provides a clear plan for each day and the power to work with other people in complete unity. In a time of listening God takes away fear and fortifies against uncertainty, hardship or bereavement; He gives foresight and cool judgment; He offers limitless reserves of energy and initiative.

A British General who has fought through two wars said this: "Telephone wires may be cut, wireless stations may be destroyed, but no bombardment can stop messages from God coming through if we are willing to receive them. To listen to God and obey Him is the highest form of national service for everybody everywhere."

E. W. MUNFORD, *Constable of Hungerford.*

THOS. SANDELL, *Town Trustee, Chairman N.F.U. Newbury.*

J. R. BROWN, *Town Trustee.*

S. R. NEATE, *Town Trustee.*

T. W. ALEXANDER, *Town Trustee, J.P. (Berks).*

H. L. PERCY, B.Sc., *Town Trustee, A.R.P. Controller.*

E. S. GINGELL, *Town Trustee, Vice-Chairman Parish Council.*

W. S. RAINE, O.B.E., *Town Trustee, Food Control Officer.*

E. F. JAMES, *Town Trustee.*

H. E. PHILLIPS, *J.P., Chairman R.D.C.,*
County Chairman Public Assistance and Public Health

MARY P. NEATE, *J.P.*

CAPTAIN A. C. BURMESTER, *J.P.*

PIN THIS UP IN YOUR HOME.   Further copies may be had from the Constable of Hungerford.

178. Advice from the Constable, c1940

Until the formation of the Town Council in 1974, Hungerford's leading citizen had been the Constable. Here Mr Ernest Munford, who ran the printing works, printed an advice sheet for the citizens of Hungerford on how to behave during the war. On 1st February 1940 he also sent out the following missive to all homes in Hungerford: 'Dear Sir or Madam, We are all cold and uncomfortable. The soldiers in our Town are much worse than we are. Can you help by offering one or more hot baths a week? A cup of tea afterwards would make it a grand treat. Please return the enclosed post card as soon as possible. Yours faithfully, E Munford'.

179. Hungerford Auxiliary Fire Service, 1936

This picture, taken in Barr's Yard (behind 5 High Street), shows the AFS in their latest fast-response vehicle – a Ford V8. What style?! The driver is Tom Cox; Officer in Charge Jack Brewer; in the rear seat are Jack Sadler and Bert Wyatt; standing is Tup Lambourne, and in the rear seat is Charles Williams.

180. 'Wings for Victory' parade, 2 May 1943

Fighting wars is a very expensive business. In addition to massive loans from the United States, the government devised many ways to encourage the average person in the street to invest their money in Savings Bonds, Savings Certificates, Savings Stamps, Post Office and Trustee Savings Banks. The scheme worked, and by 1945 savings bonds had raised £1,745 million for the war effort. Campaigns included 'War Weapons Week', 'Warship Week', 'Wings for Victory' and 'Salute the Soldier'. The photograph shows WAAFs from Ramsbury taking part in the Grand Procession on Sunday 2 May 1943, during Hungerford's 'Wings for Victory' week. Air Marshall Sir Arthur S Barret KCB CMG MC is seen here taking the Salute. The Marlborough Times reported the order of procession to be: Bren Gun Carrier; Banner (RAF); Chief Marshall; Band of Bomber Command; Contingent of RAF; Contingent of RAF Regiment; Contingent of WAAFS; Royal Observer Corp; Band of ATC; Contingent of ATC; Contingent of Royal Marine Engineers; Band of Border Regiment; Contingent of Royal Ulster Rifles; New Zealand Forces; Pioneer Corps; Band of Home Guard; Contingent of Home Guard; British Legion. The banner on the bridge reads 'OUR SPITS TO BEAT FRITZ. £50,000 FOR TEN SPITFIRES'.

181. HMS Freesia K43
1940-1947

A little earlier in the war, Hungerford adopted a warship, the Flower Class corvette HMS Freesia K43. £90,000 was raised in Hungerford and district in 'Warship Week' in 1941 to pay for the Freesia. Flower class ships were small convoy escort vessels armed with one 4 inch gun, a crew of 70, and reached a speed of 16 knots. Almost 300 were built during the 1939-45 war. The Freesia was laid down on 18th June 1940 at Harland & Wolff in Belfast, launched just 15 weeks later on 3 October, and went into service on 19 November. Flower class corvettes were convoy escort boats, capable of being built quickly, of mounting the then available anti-submarine equipment, of surviving the heavy seas around the British Isles, and of matching U-boat speeds. 145 Flower class corvettes were eventually built, and they inflicted considerable damage to attacking U-boats, sinking over 50 enemy submarines. On 12 December 1942, HMS Freesia (under Lt RA Cherry, RNR) helped to pick up 44 survivors when the British merchant Empire Gull was torpedoed and sunk west of Maputo, Portuguese East Africa. The original captain Commander Crick lived to the age of 95 years, and died in 1997. The crew visited Hungerford in 1946. In July 1946 HMS Freesia was sold to the merchant fleet and sunk on 1 April 1947.

182. General Eisenhower on Hungerford Common, 10 August 1944

Just two months after D-Day, there were huge numbers of American troops around Hungerford, on 10 August about 18,000 gathered on Hungerford Common for a parade in front of General Eisenhower, the Allied Supreme Commander. The entire 101st Airborne Division was present (13,000 men), as well as large representatives from nearby US air bases. The following is an extract from a diary written by Barney Welton, a pilot with the 436th Troop Carrier Group stationed at Membury. 'We arose at 5:30am, August 10, dressed in pinks and drove to Hungerford Park. There was a parade of 18,000 soldiers of Troop Carrier Command and 101st Airborne Division. General Eisenhower himself presented many with decorations and then made a short speech. He promised us big doings soon here and in the south Pacific and announced the formation of the 1st Airborne Command made up of us in Troop Carrier, the 101st Airborne Division, 82nd Airborne Division and 6th British Airborne, under the command of General Brereton'. This command was officially called The First Allied Airborne Army and its new commander had formerly been in charge of the US Ninth Air Force. General Eisenhower is pictured here pinning the Distinguished Service Cross on 1st Lt Walter G Amerman of the 506th Parachute Infantry Regiment for bravery during action in Normandy.

183 & 184. Regent cinema c1950 and c1953

The Regent cinema was built in 1934 by J Wooldridge & Sons (of the wharf) on land in Church Way, at the top of Atherton Hill (always known as 'Picture Hill'). It was owned by Miss Moore from Wantage, and opened on 22 November 1934; Lily Ruddle (later Mrs Griffith) became cashier in January 1935. Prior to this, films were regularly shown in the Corn Exchange (see plate 3).

During the war, the cinema was always packed with troops of all nationalities, evacuees from the cities, as well as people working in the area, but living away from home. It was one of the few places of entertainment in the area. The Regent cinema became unprofitable in the 1960s, closed in 1972, and was demolished the following year, the houses of Regent Close being built on the site.

185. Our Lady of Lourdes Catholic church, c1945

In March 1907 a new sanitary inspector was appointed in Hungerford – Mr William Strickland, who was a devout Catholic. At that time there was no Catholic church in Hungerford, and he (and others) had to travel to attend mass in Newbury, or occasionally in the chapel at Inglewood House. Over the years a parish community built up, and requests were made to the bishop to have a proper church built. The opportunity came in 1939, when a pre-fabricated building in London became available. Many sites for the church were explored, but eventually it was agreed that it should be built on land in Priory Road owned by Mr Strickland. The building arrived on a lorry from London in July 1939; the construction work was completed in November and on Sunday 26 November 1939 at a mass said by Bishop Cotter of Portsmouth, the new Catholic church was officially blessed and dedicated to Our Lady of Lourdes. This 'temporary' building has so far provided excellent service for nearly 70 years!

186 & 187. St John's mission hall, c1900 and 1984

The Mission Hall (see plate 130) had been built in 1899, and was long used by the Church Army. It was in regular use until it closed in 1984, and the site later redeveloped as St John's Court.

188 & 189. Ottermill Chilton factory, Church Way c1975

There were many entrepreneurs during the Second World War. Locally, two very bright young students at the De Havilland Technical School, the Hon AH Dalrymple and Mr 'Reggie' Ward (son of the Hon Sir John Ward of Chilton Lodge) were two such entrepreneurs. Along with their woodworking instructor at De Havilland, Mr Fred Luscombe, they went on to design their own aircraft, the Chilton Monoplane, and they formed, on 18 May 1936, Chilton Aircraft, using a specially constructed wooden building on the Ward's estate at Chilton Lodge.

The first prototype made its inaugural flight on 16 April 1937. In 1941 they went over to manufacturing small machined metal parts for the war effort, under sub-contract to larger firms. Having started in 1938 with two men and a boy, by 1945 it was employing around 250 people working shifts around the clock. Chilton aircraft went on to make a large number of monoplanes, and sailplanes, but with the death of Andrew Dalrymple on Christmas Day 1945, aircraft manufacture came to an end at Chilton. The firm switched to a rapidly expanding electrical business, including electric shavers, circuit breakers, hair clippers, the first-ever spin dryers in the UK, and the famous bathroom shaver sockets, of which 2,500,000 were made and exported world-wide.

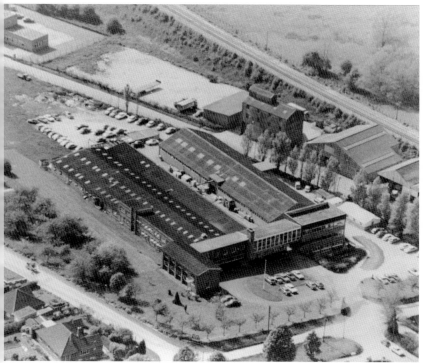

By the mid 1950s the buildings at Chilton Lodge had become totally inadequate, and a new factory was built in Hungerford. Chilton Aircraft became Chilton Electric Products, which occupied the new factory building in July 1959. At its peak in the mid 1960s there were over 400 people on the Chilton group payroll. In 1969 it became Ottermill Chilton, and in the mid 1970s it was taken over by the Westinghouse Corporation. During the mid 1980s they transferred all the manufacturing to Ireland, and sadly the factory closed in November 1985, the site being sold for housing (Cherry Grove).

190 & 191. King & Queen receiving the Lancastrian rose, 12 March 1948

Tradition has it that ever since the time of John of Gaunt, whenever the monarch has passed through Hungerford, he or she has been presented with a Lancastrian red rose. When people in Hungerford heard on 12 March that the King and Queen were visiting Marlborough College that day, a telegram was sent at noon stating that 'it would give the inhabitants of Hungerford great pleasure if His Majesty would stop for two minutes on his return journey to receive the traditional red rose – Constable of Hungerford.' A reply came at 12.54 from the Equerry, stating that they would be pleased to stop. Urgent plans were made to obtain a red rose – which eventually arrived from London by train! Word spread rapidly around the town, and by the time the Royal car came into sight at 5.20pm, the whole of Charnham Street around The Bear Hotel was packed with adults and children. It is said there was a crowd of 800 people. The King and Queen are seen here talking with the Constable Roy Alexander and the Town Clerk, Mr Angus Marshall. Within a few minutes, the Royal party continued on their way to Windsor Castle.

192. Queen's Coronation, June 1953

These splendid decorations on the railway bridge were designed and built by Roy Bennett, agricultural engineers in Charnham Street. On the left is a large electrical transformer. On the right, outside Kennet House 19 High Street, is the Sunbeam Talbot that belonged to Mr Ernest James, 'the Governor' who owned James Mill.

193. Munford's printers, June 1953

The whole town was decorated to celebrate the Coronation. Here is Ernest Munford's printers, (until recently Walton's Clothing).

194. Hungerford Carnival 1954

Annual carnivals were interrupted by the war, but they were restarted in 1953, triggered by the Queen's Coronation. The specific aim of the carnival was to raise enough money to build a new outdoor swimming pool for the town.

195. Hungerford Carnival c1956 One of the fund-raisers was the 'Lump of Coal' competition. A huge lump of coal is on the lorry outside Roy Alexander's coal merchant's shop, 120 High Street (now 'Hello Flower' florists). Roy Alexander is standing outside his shop with tickets in hand; Miss Bell, who sold pet foods and took coal orders is proudly posed for the picture. The competition cost 3d a guess. The prize . . ? 'Guess the weight, and win the lump!'. This one weighed in at 14 cwt.

196, 197, 198. Open-air swimming pool

When the carnivals restarted in 1953, the main aim was to raise funds for a new open-air swimming pool. It took some years to arrange, but the pool was built near the new Priory estate and opened in 1964 under the chairmanship of Mrs Becky Kennedy. With the exception of the first few months, it was run for its whole duration by Ken and Liz Hall. The aerial photograph shows (from left to right) the football ground, the children's playground, the War Memorial Avenue and the swimming pool.

The popularity of the swimming-pool varied according to the weather, but on good days it was enjoyed by very large numbers of children and adults. In addition to the main pool with a small diving platform, there was a small toddlers' pool, and later on a large area of grass was made available for sunbathing or playing ball games and table tennis. The pool closed in 1997 and the land used for a skateboard park.

199. Cycle speedway track, 1964

Near to the swimming pool was the cycle speedway track, which opened c1955.

Cycle racing was very popular, and a group of locals who used to travel to Swindon speedway track formed the Hungerford 'Panthers', run by Bert and Mandy Mansbridge. This photograph shows a race taking place on the August Bank Holiday, 1964. In the background are the tennis court, cricket pitch and football ground.

200. Hungerford's auxiliary and volunteer firemen, 1941/2

The Auxiliary Fire Service members (in caps) and the Hungerford
Volunteer Fire Brigade members (in helmets), arranged in front of
the Leyland fire appliance in the Bear Hotel yard. In this picture are
23 men – From left to right: front row – Tom Cox, Bob Moffatt,
Stan Poulton, Bert Wyatt, Bill Cox, Jack Brewer; second row – Jim
Woods, Charlie Geater, Jack Morley, Tup Lambourne, Jack Pike,
Vic Caswell, Old Ted Stevens; third row – Con Wilkins, Tom
Buckland, Reg Honeybone, Alf Macklin, Doug Wilmott, George
Willis; back row – Ted Stevens, Bob Fisher, Reg Whiscombe,
Harry Giles.

201 & 202. Fire at Great Western Mill, Church Street, 22 June 1960

The large steel-framed, asbestos-clad Great Western Mill in Church Street (see plate 155) had been opened in 1932. On the night of 22 June 1960, however, a devastating fire razed the building despite the best efforts of ten fire tenders in Church Street, a further ten pumping water, and three turntable ladders. As well as the Hungerford crews, appliances came from Newbury, Lambourn, Wantage, Didcot, Mortimer, Pangbourne, Reading, Ramsbury and Marlborough. Parts of the building continued to smoulder for eight weeks.

203. The new Great Western Mill, Smitham Bridge, 1974

James & Co spared no time in forging ahead with building a new bigger and more modern mill a little further from the town centre at Smitham Bridge. By early September outline plans were submitted and had been passed by the Rural District Council. Building work started in January 1961, and the new mill opened in January 1962. The family ownership ended in 1964, the business continuing through a number of ever-larger commercial take-overs. Eventually, in the early 1980s it was owned by Dalgety, but they chose to close the New Mill in Hungerford in June 1984, the site being sold to Trencherwoods, who started the housing development of Pound Piece, Wessex Close, Somerset Close and Wiltshire Close in 1986.

204. The fire station, Church Street, 1991

When the fire destroyed the Great Western Mill in Church Street, the James family built the 'New Mill' at Smitham Bridge. The vacant site in Church Street was made available for the present library (first built 1967, re-built 2007), fire station (1968) and car park.

205. New railway bridge over the High Street, 1966

Great excitement (and huge disruption to traffic!) came when the railway
bridge across the High Street was replaced. The first bridges across roads in
the town were erected in 1862 when the single track line was extended
from Hungerford to Seend near Devizes. The line was changed to double-
track requiring new bridges in 1896, and this lattice sided bridge features in
many of the photographs in this book. It needed replacing in 1966, and it
is said that this is the longest span of any railway bridge on the Great
Western Railway network.

206 & 207. Petrol station on Manor House site, c1968

After the surgery had moved from the High Street to The Croft in 1959, an
extraordinary planning decision resulted in the historic Manor House being
demolished in 1965, the site then being converted for use as a petrol station
run by Bill Norman. The new (1968) railway bridge can be seen in place.
The petrol station closed in 1970, and a new International Stores
supermarket built on the site. (Redeveloped 1999 into the access road to
Somerfield car park, and a retail shop, until recently African Trackwoods).

208. The Croft surgery, 1975

When the lease on Manor House in the High Street (see plate 161) was ending, Drs Max Wallis and Robert Kennedy decided to build a new purpose-designed surgery in The Croft. This was one of the first purpose-built surgeries in the country, and it opened in 1959. There was space for three doctors, as well as the waiting-room and a small office. This photograph shows the surgery in 1973 (with the old semaphore railway signal behind). General practice has changed much since 1973, and after several modest extensions to the building in the 1970s and 80s, the building was doubled in size in 1993.

209. Hungerford hospital c1988

The Hungerford and Ramsbury Union workhouse was built on open land on the south side of Cow Lane (now Park Street) in 1847. It was of the 'Stratton' design (named after Stratton St Margaret near Swindon). With the establishment of the NHS it became Hungerford hospital, and eventually a psycho-geriatric unit as part the Fairmile Hospital group. The number of patients reduced during the 1980s, and Hungerford hospital closed in 1989. The buildings were eventually demolished in November 1995, the area being redeveloped for Ramsbury Drive and Aldbourne Close.

210. John O'Gaunt school, 1964

By the early 1960s, the council school buildings in Fairview Road, dating from 1910, were bursting with over 530 pupils. The planned solution was a newly built secondary modern school on the southern edge of the town, and the John of Gaunt school (later re-named John O'Gaunt) opened in 1963. 290 pupils transferred, and the council school in Fairview Road became the primary school. The John O'Gaunt became a comprehensive school, and is now a community technology college, linked to nine feeder primary schools in the area.

211 & 212. The Croft nursery school, 1981 and 1988

This pre-fabricated building opened in 1942 as a wartime nursery (later re-named day nursery) administered by the Ministry of Health, to provide young mothers with crèche facilities whilst they worked at local factories involved in the war effort, including the Vickers Armstrong aircraft factory in Eddington and the Chilton aircraft factory. The nursery was open from 7am until 7pm, and as well as providing meals (including breakfast), the emphasis was on health and cleanliness. The day nursery closed for a short time in 1946, but re-opened as a nursery school on 9 December 1947, now under the Ministry of Education.

Many nursery schools were closed during the 1950s, but Hungerford's was retained, and shone as an example of the best of pre-school learning by experiment in a happy atmosphere. Learning about health was always important – toothbrush drill and handkerchief drill were on the timetable! The nursery school flourished under excellent head teachers, and when the 'temporary' building, which had an intended life of ten years when it was erected in 1942, eventually came to the end of its useable life, Hungerford was fortunate that the nursery school was replaced by a grand new building, which opened in January 2005.

213. Hungerford West signal box c1912

The railway goods yard at Hungerford (to the east of the station buildings) was a very busy yard until the 1950s. To support all the activity in the area, there were two signal boxes in the early 20th century, Hungerford East (seen in plate 37) and the West box seen in this photograph adjacent to the level crossing by the station. When the East box closed in 1939, the West box took over all the local traffic.

214-216. Railway crash, 10 November 1971

In the early morning of Wednesday 10 November 1971, a goods train from Westbury to Theale, with 41 wagons containing 1000 tons of stone, was de-railed whilst on the high embankment just west of the High Street bridge. Most of the wagons piled together at the station, and the signal box was nearly demolished. Despite such a catastrophic crash, it is remarkable that no-one was injured, although the signalman, Bob Bowden, was trapped in his signal box for over half an hour until rescued by firemen. After the crash, a temporary box was built on the west end of the up platform, but this too was removed when colour light signals replaced semaphore signals in July 1978.

217. Councillors of Hungerford, 1979

Major changes in local government were introduced in England and Wales in 1974 - larger parish councils were given the option to become Town Councils. Hungerford, which had always considered itself a town, accepted the challenge, and the chairman of the new Town Council became the Mayor. This historic photograph was taken in 1979 on the occasion of the retirement of longstanding councillors Charles Williams (28 years service) and Gerry Watson (30 years service). It shows 17 councillors, and includes no fewer than nine Mayors and Parish Council Chairmen. Hungerford's first Mayor, Joe Brady, had died in office. From left to right: Bill Acworth (Town Councillor); Lord Edmund Fermoy (Mayor 1982/83); John McCubbin (County & Town Councillor); John Hathway (Mayor 1985/86); Hugh Hassall (Mayor 1984/85); Chris Brown (Mayor 1983/84); Mrs Becky Kennedy (Chairman 1970/74); Ernie Whittaker (Mayor 1981/82); Charles Williams (Town Councillor); Vic Lardner (Town Councillor); Jack Williams (Chairman 1965/69, Mayor 1978/81); Bert King (former District Council chairman); Rev Charles Gill (Town Councillor); Jean Tubb (Town Councillor); Ron Tarry (Mayor 1976/77 and 1987/88); Frank Light (District & Town Councillor); Gerry Watson (Chairman 1960/61); and Beryl Fowler (Town Clerk). Collectively, the councillors in the photograph contributed well over 300 years of service to the town of Hungerford.

218. The library, Church Street, 2007
The purpose-built library in Church Street first opened in 1967, on land made available after the fire at James' Mill. It was refurbished in 1987 but after discussion in 2005, plans were made to build a new bigger and better facility. The 1967 library and the adjacent public toilets were demolished in March 2007, and building work is proceeding rapidly. The new library is planned to open in the autumn of 2007.

219. Re-opening of the canal 20 July 1974
The Kennet and Avon Canal was originally opened to Hungerford on 9 October 1798, and the first barge to the wharf is reported as 'having on board a staircase of Portland stone for J Pearse, Esq, of Chilton Lodge, several casks of Russian tallow . . . making the whole about 40 tons weight.' The opening of the Great Western Railway in 1841 meant that canal trade declined - it never made a profit after 1877, and fell into disrepair during the 20th century. When the canal was restored, and re-opened to Hungerford in 1974 a large crowd gathered on a glorious July day. As the official barge came into sight there was great anticipation – but the barge grounded under the canal bridge for a worrying few minutes! Thankfully, it was soon freed, and the official reception on the wharf went ahead, where the dignitaries were greeted by the Constable, Mr John Newton. Perhaps this day more than any other marked the beginning of Hungerford's tourist era. As we now move on through the 21st century, the town, the canal and the beautiful surrounding countryside continue to be enjoyed by residents and visitors alike.